Sparrow

ALSO BY JAN RICHARDSON

The Cure for Sorrow
Circle of Grace
Through the Advent Door
In the Sanctuary of Women
In Wisdom's Path
Night Visions
Sacred Journeys

sparrow

A Book *of* Life *and* Death *and* Life

JAN RICHARDSON

Wanton Gospeller Press
ORLANDO, FLORIDA

janrichardson.com   wantongospeller.com

FOR GARY

The beating of your heart
your brightest song

Contents

Introduction

It began as a list, a record, a reckoning.
   It became a lament, a liturgy.
   It became a conversation.
   It became a testimony and a prayer.
   It became a nest.

It began when my husband went into the hospital one autumn
day for what we had anticipated would be the successful repair of
a brain aneurysm. During Gary's surgery, a clot appeared, causing
a massive stroke. A medical coma ensued, along with many procedures and two further surgeries in the days that followed.

   As we kept vigil, I opened a file on my laptop and began making notes. I wanted to keep track of what was unfolding: procedures
and surgeries, medications and tests, names of the staff who cared
for him, family and friends who came to wait with us. I wrote down
the things I would tell Gary when he woke, things I would want
him to know about what had happened while he was sleeping.

   Gary did not wake. As the complications cascaded and hope
began to erode, I stopped writing. Seventeen days after his initial
surgery, on the second day of Advent, Gary died.

   On a summer evening six months after Gary's death, I opened
the file I had started after his surgery. I began to write again. As I
had done before, I wrote in the second person, to Gary, the *you* to

whom I had written in the hospital. I set out not knowing where I was going and not at all certain there was still a *you* who remained, who endured, who knew anything of what I was writing to him.

The pages became a secret space of struggle and lament, a hidden shelter where I could tell of the bewilderment, the grinding sense of absence, the questions that attended me, the moments of connection and beauty that found their way into the chaos of grief. The pages became a place to tell of the strange occasions of synchronicity, the workings of dreams, and the surprising stubbornness of hope. They became a place of solace, of sheltering. They became a refuge and a nest.

I had not set out to build a nest, but it should perhaps have come as no surprise that in the profound sense of un-homing that came with Gary's death, a nest was what showed up. Gary and I had shared a particular fondness for Psalm 84, where the psalmist offers a beautiful and compelling image of what it means to look for home:

> My soul longs, indeed it faints
> for the courts of the LORD;
> my heart and my flesh sing for joy
> to the living God.

> Even the sparrow finds a home,
> and the swallow a nest for herself,
> where she may lay her young,
> at your altars, O LORD of hosts.

The psalm was a favorite also of the early Celtic monks, many of whom spent their lives in *peregrinatio*, the practice of perpetual pilgrimage. It was easy for us to imagine their fondness for the psalm—that it spoke to those who had released their claim on any earthly home and who instead found their home in God. It spoke also to the home Gary and I had found in each other.

The psalm inspired one of Gary's most beautiful songs. "I Will Be a Sparrow" draws upon those lovely home-finding, nest-building images that open the psalm. It draws, too, from lines in the psalm that tell of a valley where tears become springs, the traveler goes from strength to strength, and joy finds its way. When it came time to choose a song to play at the beginning of Gary's memorial service, this was the one that kept coming to mind. As it played, his words rang with a prescience both comforting and strange:

Until I appear before you
I will be a sparrow
In the house of God
I will be a sparrow
And the altar of the Lord
Will be my home

In the months that followed, sparrows began to show up with odd frequency, as if the sparrow of Gary's song were winging through the devastation that his death had brought to my life. The sparrows took not just physical form, flitting across my path as I navigated a world so altered by his absence; they found their way to me by other means as well, slipping into conversations, poems, books.

I was reluctant to take the sparrows as signs. But the sparrows' persistence became hard to ignore, the sense of being attended difficult to escape. I began to think of their presence simply as a witness to the mystery that moves in the deepest loss.

Even as the sparrows became an unexpected source of solace, they reminded me of Jesus' words in Matthew's Gospel, where he says, *Are not two sparrows sold for a penny? Yet not one of them will fall to the ground apart from your Father* (10:29). His words of comfort hold a harrowing reality: the sparrow still falls.

These pages are, in part, a testimony to that reality and to the wrestling I've had to do with it. I am not interested in trying to make it make sense. I simply want to attend to the terrible fall and give it the lamentation it deserves.

I had begun these pages out of necessity, out of desperation. As I continued to write, a vocabulary started to emerge, a language that could articulate not only my loss but also the love that endured beneath and beyond that loss: the love that was fiercer still than my grief.

With the arrival of language came a sense of something happening that felt like a conversation. *Conversation* is perhaps an overly precise word for a wildly imprecise experience. An exchange; an engagement; a connection woven of impression and intuition, synchronicity and poetry and dream—whatever it was, it was something other than the seeming void that had opened with Gary's death. I found myself thinking of the first time he and I had talked, how it felt like we were picking up a conversation that had already been going on forever. I began to sense the conversation was not finished but taking place now in a radically altered form.

In time, as the pages gathered, I began to wonder if they were meant for more than just Gary and me—if perhaps there was a bigger nest here, an invitation to open up the conversation and the sheltering I had found. *Sparrow* is the result of this wondering.

I have worked with the original text, shaping the conversation into something that can be shared. I have left out pieces and let some details stand without trying to explain them—people, events, and places that have been part of the weave of my life, the description of which would have become unwieldy. I think again of a nest, how its gaps are a necessary part of its structure, how its shelter depends in part on what is hidden from view.

When I began writing those first pages in the hospital, I had hoped this would be a different kind of record of repair. What I had thought would be an accounting of Gary's restoration and healing became a search for my own.

The search has gone in anything but a straight line. Far from being a progressive process, grief moves by turns and spirals, a twisting path that I am not sure can even be called a path because it is not always that clear or orderly. Grief is the least linear thing I know.

The unpredictable and circuitous nature of grief offers a paradoxical, if unsought, freedom and grace. If sorrow gives us no straightforward or prescribed road, no standard manual for its healing, then we are not bound to travel it by a way that does not fit for us.

What we are bound to is love: the love that gives rise to our grief but finally goes deeper than it, the love that undergirds and carries us through every turning. As we learn to navigate our sorrow, love gives us the tools we need—the language, the images, the remedies, the particular forms of solace by which our particular hearts will find repair.

I have found the most compelling repairs are the ones that make themselves visible, that leave evidence of the breakage and also of the imagination by which the breakage becomes transformed. Such repairs are always provisional, imperfect, and ongoing. Like a nest, they involve continual mending. They ask for a willingness to keep remaking what is perpetually at risk of falling apart. It is this remaking by which a home, and a life, may come: not in spite of what has gone before, but because of it.

I Will Be a Sparrow

To be a pilgrim
Have the road that leads to you
In my heart and in my mind
Find these pools of blessing
Along the dusty way
The driest vale wet with tears of joy

Hear my prayer, Almighty
You are my only strength
Until I appear before you
I will be a sparrow
In the house of God
I will be a sparrow
And the altar of the Lord
Will be my home

To be in your house
Within your shelter
Peace within your walls
No other home have I
In all the world
No other home do I seek

Hear my prayer, Almighty
You are my only strength
Until I appear before you
I will be a sparrow
In the house of God
I will be a sparrow
And the altar of the Lord
Will be my home

—Garrison Doles

PART ONE
If You Abide

THE QUESTION

If the answer is yes,
send one sparrow.

If no,
send two.

—Tuesday, June 3, 2014—
Home*

Oh, my love.

You are six months gone as of yesterday. I have wanted to write to you over the past months—and have not wanted to write. There are so many gaps, and I am wrenched by them: wrenched by the gaps I won't be able to fill about what happened (there was so much of it), wrenched by how overwhelming it seems to even try.

When you were still in the hospital, I was wishing I had started writing to you sooner, had kept better track of details, even a few sentences about what unfolded each day. I made a start, but in the midst of all that was going on every day and every hour in the hospital, in that awful and beautiful vigil we kept, it seemed quickly to become overwhelming to write down even a few words, and I feel failure in that.

I think of the writer—I think it was Anne Lamott—I heard say, years ago, that there were days when she had to trick herself into writing by telling herself, *If I can just sit down and write one square inch.* Maybe if I can write one square inch at a time, I can find my way into this, can begin to feel my way around the gaps, if not fill them, after these months that have passed. Knowing I won't remember everything. Knowing, as with so many of the gaps I'm coming up against, I'm going to have to learn to be okay with that.

Not knowing just what I am trying to do here, on this page. But needing somehow to be present to the story—your story—in ways that will happen only in laying words down on the page. Knowing that words aren't enough, that words aren't everything. Knowing some relief in this: that even if I had all the words I needed, they wouldn't hold the whole story. Your story. Ours.

One square inch. But how deep, how achingly deep the grief that lies beneath that one square inch. Bottomless.

For today, I will tell you this. Today I made a trip to the library to return a few books and pick up more. I found my way to the

---

**Unless otherwise indicated, entries were written at home.*

nonfiction section, where I rarely go when I'm in that branch, given how small that section is. Was curious to see what they might have by way of poetry. Not much, not surprisingly. But just next to the poetry, there was a book whose title caught my eye: *Call If You Need Me*. I pulled it from the shelf. Found it was a collection of stories by Raymond Carver, who seems to have become our friend of late. I noticed it was just three books up from a popular book about grief that I had heard referenced many times in the past few years but had never picked up. I picked it up today, skimmed through it, read a few sections. Felt a suffocating sensation in my chest. *Not for me, not for me*, I thought. *Not now, at least.*

It's a recurring motif: skip the books on grief; pick up the poetry (or the fiction). Struck by how very close those two books, Carver's and the other, were to one another on the shelf today, as if highlighting for me, underscoring, emphasizing: *This, not that.*

—Wednesday, June 4, 2014—

After you died, I quickly discovered it was nearly impossible for me to make plans very far in advance. Felt like I could do about fifteen minutes at a time. Getting a little better at it, but it's still challenging. Hard to know what I'm going to be up for. Typically I don't press it, don't pressure myself to feel like I have to make plans. But I made plans as June 2 approached, knowing I would need something in place for the day that marked six months since you died.

I went over to Janice's for lunch. Janice. Thank God for Janice, who is so *Janice*, and I know you know what I mean. Janice, who knew each of us before we knew each other and who played a significant part in our getting together.

So, lunch at Janice's, in her and Seth's lovely home, where you and I spent a number of New Year's Eves. I hadn't been over there since my last New Year's Eve with you. Janice remembers how you and I danced in her kitchen.

Lunch was lovely. We talked and cried over cheese and olives and wine for some time, then had the yummy soup she had made.

And we remembered. I couldn't tell you much of what we talked about, just that it was good to talk.

I think Janice cried more than I did. It's often like that with folks; they cry because they feel for me or because it reminds them of their own sorrow over you. But for me, the sorrow is always there, always so present, varying from sharp to aching and back to sharp again. I weep frequently when I am alone—because I am so alone—and when I am with others, feel more reserved, or more spent from the tears. Though the tears do come with them, sometimes, but mostly when I'm on my own.

I was late to Janice's. Though I had been awake for hours, having awakened, maddeningly, long before I needed to, I was having such a hard time getting my act together that morning and wound up arriving around 1:00 when I had planned to be there at 12:30. I had an appointment scheduled with Christianne at three. Janice had made a rustic pie and suggested I stop back by after my appointment, as Christianne lives—literally—just two minutes from her, and I could also pick up the blue hydrangeas that she had picked and arranged for me from her beautiful garden.

Christianne. My first time at her and Kirk's home. They live in a cottage in a beautiful neighborhood of big, fancy Winter Park homes. I think they probably have the best place of all. They rent their cottage from the folks in the big house next door. It looks like something out of a fairy tale. Christianne said that a niece of Thomas Edison used to live there, long ago. She was an artist and painted the doors and cabinets in a wonderful folk art style. It's a marvelous space, cozy and welcoming. I've recently made arrangements with Christianne to see her once a week for spiritual direction.

This was our second visit; for our first one, a couple of weeks ago, I invited her to come over here so that she could see the home you and I had created together, especially before I begin sorting your studio—whenever that happens. It is not happening as soon as I thought it would, and I am okay with that.

The space with her feels exactly right so far. It feels like good timing. It feels like a huge relief—to know that once a week, there's a place where I can go to talk and talk and talk, to spill some of my story and our story, and to know it will be heard and held and that she'll help me listen to the story, to our story; will help me know what pieces I need to attend to; will help me listen my way into whatever life is unfolding before me now.

I'm curious about how Christianne—and Kirk too—came into my life, into our lives. We met them on the Audire retreat we led in 2012 and felt a connection. The four of us had talked about getting together, and Christianne and I had talked about the two of us having a visit over tea, and somehow none of that happened. But they often came to Wellspring, and it always made my heart glad to see them. After they heard what happened with your surgery, Christianne sent me a text, saying to let her know if I needed someone to come sit with me at the hospital.

That night of your third and final surgery—after Janice had left, after sitting with me for hours all through the surgery, and having a meal afterward—I found myself alone and shaky. It was probably around eight o'clock at night when I called Christianne, told her about the surgery, told her that you were stable but that I was not. *Do you remember how you said if I needed someone?* And she came, and she brought some of the dinner she had made for her and Kirk that evening. And banana bread. And we sat in your room and talked for a bit, then went down to the end of the hall and talked a bit more. She's one of the only people outside of our family I let into your room.

She and Kirk came to your memorial service, and they came to the Wellspring service just a few days later—the Advent Wellspring service. I had gotten in touch with her beforehand to ask if she could come a little early to help me set up, but mostly it was because I wanted someone there, didn't want to be in the chapel by myself. Turns out that several people, on their own beautiful initiative, came early to help. So grateful.

I thought often of Christianne after that, wanting to meet but somehow not managing to do it. And think it's one of those cases where that was okay, and perhaps just right. Finally arranged to have lunch about three weeks ago. We met at Infusion Tea. She was already there when I arrived and had snagged the big table in the back corner. I felt such relief in her presence.

For months, prior to having lunch with Christianne, I had been thinking I might benefit from talking with someone on a regular basis. I thought that probably meant a therapist, and over the past months I had done some asking around to see if any of my friends knew someone they thought might be a good fit. A number of names came to the surface, and there were a couple of people I had considered calling, but every time, when it came down to it, I hesitated. In the few days before I saw Christianne, I had gained some clarity about what I was looking for and had started to think perhaps what I needed fell more into the category of spiritual direction than therapy. On my way home, after having lunch with Christianne, I began to wonder if she was a person who could provide the kind of space I need right now. That wondering lingered with me over the days that followed.

The next week, I sent her an email asking if she would be willing to do some spiritual direction with me. Shared some of what I sensed I was needing. *An intentional and regular space*, I wrote, *to talk about Gary, to share some of our story, to have support as I continue to be present to what's unfolding, and to listen my way into the life that lies ahead of me.*

She wrote back saying yes. I wept when I read it, I was so relieved.

And so that space with her feels good and right and a huge step in discerning what I need and asking for it.

Grateful.

After our session, I went back to Janice's, had pie and tea and a little more visiting. She sent me home with leftover soup and pie and with the beautiful blue hydrangeas—not remembering or knowing, until I told her, that I had carried blue hydrangeas at our wedding. The ones that wilted and were replaced with ones that also wilted. Which I will try not to take as an omen in retrospect. It is good, if poignant, to have the beautiful hydrangeas in our home, bearing witness to that exquisite wedding day you and I shared, and the afternoon I spent with our dear friend Janice.

—Friday, June 6, 2014—

Scott and Lacinda spent the day here yesterday. They've been wonderful about coming down every month or so to check in on me and spend a day. We had lunch nearby at Hubbly Bubbly; their first time, my second. Tasty lunches all around.

We made a stop by the post office and then set out on our project *du jour*: shopping for a vacuum. You know how much I disliked the one you got some years ago. I think, all told, you had worked on it, I had worked on it, Lacinda had worked on it, and Craig had worked on it, and it was still lousy. We found one, a Hoover. Scott and Lacinda put it together after we got home, and I gave it a whirl. The amount of dirt it picked up just in the couple of minutes we spent testing it was a testimony to the amount of dirt that the previous vacuum had not picked up!

Scott fixed a delicious dinner (he and Lacinda had brought down seafood and other treats) while Lacinda and I went through your puzzle collection, which I had moved from the guest room to the island in your studio. At one point we were sitting on the floor of your studio, looking at the puzzles, deciding what to keep and what to give away. Tears came as I thought about all those evenings we sat together in the living room, me reading or watching television while you worked one of your puzzles. As with golf, it absorbed you in a way that relieved you from thinking about work. Thank God for puzzles and golf. I didn't have the patience to puzzle myself, though I would look over your shoulder from time to time and find the right place for a piece. But I so enjoyed your enjoyment of the puzzles.

The last one you worked is still in the living room, on the makeshift table you set up near the front door, just behind the television. I think you finished it just a day or two before you went into the hospital. It's a pleasant, painted scene of a harbor, with lots of good details. It wasn't until a month or two after you died that I noticed, as I was looking at the puzzle with Karen, that the boat in the foreground is named *Olde Sweetheart*. A cozy older couple rests together in the stern. Sweetheart, that should have been us.

I haven't had the heart to move the puzzle and take down the table. Lacinda and others have suggested gluing the puzzle and saving it. Had thought perhaps of just saving the pieces that have *Olde Sweetheart* on them. That's another detail to figure out on another day.

Karen arrived as I was writing this; she called this afternoon to see if I'd like to get together. We had a lovely evening that consisted largely of feasting on Scott and Lacinda's yummy leftovers while sitting on the front porch. Talked lots about you. Grateful for the impromptu visit and for the gift of her friendship. I talked about going through the puzzles with Lacinda, and Karen said she had a puzzle you had given her from your collection. I had forgotten that and was really glad to know. Thank you for that.

—Saturday, June 7, 2014—

As independent as I have always thought myself, I savored the ways you cared for me, and I desperately miss them. This landscape of grief has been marked by scores of decisions I have had to make for myself—sometimes with counsel, but never with yours, though I can so often imagine what you would say—and tasks I have had to take care of on my own—again, sometimes with counsel and help—but every decision and every task underscores how lonely this landscape is. I had to hire a lawn service. Have had to deal with the cable company on my own, the plumber, AAA (when the battery in your car died).

The out-of-service cable and the dead battery happened on the same day. Janice came to the rescue that day; I called her in a state, overwhelmed by the things that needed to be done (and mostly just overwhelmed; this was maybe two months after you died). She came over, and after we went to lunch, we started to jump your battery but then decided it would be simpler just to call AAA, which was a good move. While the guy tested and then replaced your battery, Janice and I sat on the porch—it was raining some—and she read a Dave Barry article to me from *The Wall Street Journal* in which Dave was writing about reclaiming manly virtues—like being able to jump a battery! It provided welcome laughter.

I have come to suspect you're still finding ways to take care of me. Most vivid was the night in January when, in the mist of a terrible bout of insomnia, I was suddenly seized by the need to go to the living room and pull a book of poetry off the shelf. Specifically, I felt the need to get the book of Raymond Carver's poems, *All Of Us*. It was a gift from you; I don't remember when. (And you can believe I have kicked myself for all the books you gave me that I meant to have you inscribe, though if that's one of my few regrets, that's doing pretty well; I treasure the inscriptions you did write.) For some reason, I had never read the book.

I brought it back to bed and started to flip past Tess Gallagher's introduction so that I could get on with the poetry, but my eye was caught by a portion of one of Ray's poems she uses near the end of the introduction. It's called "For Tess," and this is the excerpt:

> Once I lay on the bank with my eyes closed,
> listening to the sound the water made,
> and to the wind in the tops of the trees. The same wind
> that blows out on the Strait, but a different wind, too.
> For awhile I even let myself imagine that I had died –
> and that was all right, at least for a couple
> of minutes, until it really sank in: *Dead*.
> As I was lying there with my eyes closed,
> just after I'd imagined what it might be like
> if in fact I never got up again, I thought of you.
> I opened my eyes then and got right up
> and went back to being happy again.
> I'm grateful to you, you see. I wanted to tell you.

I wept upon reading it, especially the last line. Wept with sorrow but mainly with my own gratefulness for you, and with wondering whether you were in that, whether you had somehow led me to that poem and to that last line.

Just two or three weeks after you died, I went out to dinner with

Karen, Kathy, and Barbara. We came back to the house afterward for dessert. As we visited, one of them asked if I felt you with me. I was caught off guard by the question; I hadn't really considered it until then. Looking back, I think your absence felt so wrenching and my loss so total that I could hardly begin to entertain the idea that something of you might be lingering as more than a memory. I talked a little about that, how you were very present in memory but that I didn't sense you lingering otherwise.

Not long after that, Maru asked me the same question. The question began to get its hooks in me, and it became unsettling and disturbing. What if I reached out for you and you weren't there? What if I did sense something; what would I do with that?

Even as I ached—and still ache—for your presence, I knew even then that I couldn't make a life around anything of you that might linger. I did wish for the comfort of knowing that something of you abided, somewhere, as more than a memory: that there would come a day, after my own dying, when I would see you again. For a time, I was plagued by fear and anguish that were directly connected with the question of whether I sensed your presence and whether I would see you again. It was unbearable to think I might not, and I couldn't claim any real grounds for hoping I would, so complete did your absence feel.

The irony was not lost on me—that I have written and talked so much about thin places, the sheer veil between worlds, and the communion of saints, but when it came down to whether I believed there was something of you that survived and that I would meet again one day as more than a memory, I was at a loss. The notion of heaven, an afterlife, existence that somehow survives our dying—it doesn't seem logical or entirely plausible. And into that mix, for a time, came pressing and painful questions about the existence of God. I know all the questions about how a loving God can allow good people to suffer, but never before have I felt the suffering so keenly or sensed so deeply the absurdity of the brokenness of the world and God's inability or unwillingness to step in more frequently. How can there be a God when you are not in this world?

Something began to shift when Raymond Carver's poem

showed up on that insomnia-plagued night. I remember telling a couple of folks—Maru, Peg—that I didn't necessarily think of the poem, with its stunning last line, as a direct message from you but that it sure felt like somebody wanted to tell me something, wanted me to know what Ray says in that poem and to take it as a word meant for me.

Weird things keep happening with books. "For Tess" was the first and most dramatic one. I don't want to make more of those strange and lovely occurrences than is warranted, but I don't want to make less of them, either, and I've come to think of that as the greater risk right now: that in my disbelief and doubt about whether something of you survives, I might miss how you might want to show up. (And of course if you showed up, it would be through books!) Again, not in ways to build a life around but perhaps in ways that would provide comfort and assurance.

Some time after that—after Ray's poem—I told Maru one evening that my questions about whether you survived, whether I would see you again, had become less acute, less anguishing. Not simply because of the poem, though that helped. But there seemed to be something settling in, I told her; some knowing settling into my bones: that you abide, that I will know you again.

In the meantime, I try to simply listen. Not only to listen for you and whatever subtle ways you might slide into my awareness; to listen only for that, to be perpetually hoping for that, would leave me stuck. But to listen around that, to listen for what's stirring, to listen for how my life will yet unfold.

—SATURDAY, JUNE 14, 2014—

Another Saturday night. One of the times I miss you most, if it's even possible to compare. I miss you all the time. If you were here, we would be ordering pizza and watching Britcoms, as we did pretty much every Saturday night when we were home together. One of my favorite cozy traditions of ours. I ache with missing it. I can't much watch the Britcoms now, though there have been a few times

I've ordered pizza (never just for myself; too lonely): a few times with Scott and Lacinda, and also a couple of Sundays ago when Susie was here and Becky and Barbara came over for dinner.

What a week. Annual Conference began on Wednesday and finished up today. I made it there only for yesterday, for the Service of Remembrance and the memorial luncheon that followed. I had forgotten, until receiving the letter a few months ago, that the memorial service recognizes not only clergy who died in the past year but clergy spouses as well. So we remembered you there. When your photo appeared on the screen during the service, it felt like someone else's life. That couldn't be you up there. But it was, and this is, all too keenly, my life. Without you.

I was in a state much of the week, feeling a good bit of stress about the service, about Conference. I had to go shopping for a new dress, and you know how I feel about shopping. I found one. Solid black, gored so that it has some flounce.

Shopping for the dress, I thought about how one of the easiest dresses I ever bought was my wedding dress. Francesca went with me to find it. I think it wasn't all that long before the wedding, maybe six weeks or so? I had quite put it off. One day, I asked Francesca if she would help me, and she thought we should do it posthaste.

We went to only one shop. I tried on three dresses. The first one was fine—fit fine, looked very wedding dress-y, price was right, but I didn't love it. The second one hadn't grabbed me all that much on the rack, but when I tried it on and walked out of the fitting room, I think Francesca and I knew right away. I hadn't expected to find a dress I loved so much. I loved that dress, partly because it felt so *me*.

When I moved into our house—our home—I hung my dress in the doorway of my studio, where it remained. We talked about it sometimes. I didn't know what to do with it. I remember wishing I had another occasion to wear it. How could I wear a dress I liked so much (and had paid so much for) only once? Didn't know whether to save it or to give it away. So it remained on the threshold of my studio.

Maybe a couple months after you died, while Karen and I were having lunch one day at The Greek Corner (where you and I had lunch so many times), we talked about the dress. I asked her if she would keep it for me for a while. (I think Sally had suggested I ask someone to do this.) We both cried. She offered to do some research on the best way to have it cleaned, perhaps preserved. Still don't know what I'll do with it. But am grateful that it's in her keeping.

She reminded me of a day—sometime last year, I think—we had gone to lunch. When we came back to the house, somehow we got to talking about the dress, and at her encouragement I put it back on for the first time since our wedding day. And you and I danced. I had forgotten about that until Karen reminded me. Grateful for that memory of dancing with you one more time in that beautiful dress.

I remember, too, with an aching clarity, your taking that dress off me on our wedding night, slowly, until it finally gathered at our feet, pooling around us like all the time in the world.

Shopping for the dress for the Service of Remembrance, especially alone, was an awful task. It was eclipsed only by having to shop for shoes to go with it. That's part of what I hate about shopping for clothes—that they sometimes require new shoes.

All I wanted was a pair of black flats. Went to a bunch of places and finally found a pair I wasn't crazy about but were pretty much the only option I had come up with. Felt spent and demoralized, particularly with having to do this in the first place.

A session with Christianne the next day, Thursday. Had asked her if I could bring the dress and shoes with me for her opinion. Christianne shared my opinion about the shoes; not fabulous but fine. But then she brought out a pair of little black flats and said I could borrow them if I'd like. Told her I should have skipped all the shopping and just come to her house!

When I left her house after our session, borrowed shoes in

hand, I had planned to let that be an end of it, to take her up on her offer and stop shopping already. At the last minute, I turned right on 17-92 and ended up at the shoe store in Fern Park where Christianne had bought her pair—not far from my old place in Maitland—and noticed a used bookstore had gone in next door.

I decided I wasn't up for a browse—very weary at that point in the week—but after picking up my own pair of the shoes Christianne had lent me, I paused at the cart of books outside the store. There was a woman on the other side of the cart; I hadn't looked closely until she said, *I know you*. It turned out to be someone I had met years ago through a committee I was on.

She told me that her husband died two months ago, and that began quite a conversation. When she began to talk about hearing "His Eye Is On the Sparrow" on the radio shortly after he died and seeing three sparrows together one day, I could hardly believe it; that we two, who had so recently lost our husbands, should have crossed paths that day and that she would talk about sparrows, which hold such significance for me, with you. I told her this, and when she asked me to explain, I shared just a little: about Psalm 84 and your song "I Will Be a Sparrow," which I had chosen as the song to play as we gathered for your memorial service in December.

Is this the kind of thing you orchestrate? I had just been talking with Christianne about how I think part of my challenge is to be open to how you might want to show up. But I have also talked with her about how I know our brains are designed to look for patterns and meanings and that, when it comes to the curious things that are happening—like with books—I don't want to make more of what's happening, to give it more significance than is warranted, but I also don't want to make less of it than I should.

I remember a conversation with Maru after stuff had begun to happen, like reading Raymond Carver's "For Tess" and beginning to feel like some knowing of you was beginning to settle into my bones. She mocked me a little, gently—that I have made so much of thin places and thresholds but could have such a hard time believing that something of you survived.

I remember also my first spiritual direction session with Maru after you died. I had invited her to come over to the house; she had never been here, and I had asked if we could have our session here, both because I anticipated it would be an emotional session and because I wanted her to see the home we had made together. I told her about going outside one afternoon. At that moment, the big oak tree in our front yard was filled with birds. So very many. I had never seen so many birds in that tree. I think they were sparrows, and one yellow warbler—which I don't recall having seen before. I had wondered, *Is this how you work now? Sending me a tree full of sparrows?* I told Maru I wasn't sure that was how things really worked. And she said, *Why not?*

I think about that again as I remember crossing paths with the woman on Thursday—after so many years and after both our husbands had died. And hearing her talking about sparrows. I wonder, *Is this you?* Is this you, orchestrating things? Wanting me to know that you are stirring? I hear Maru's gentle mocking and the words I had just shared with Christianne about sensing my resistance wearing away—my resistance to the possibility that something of you survives and wants me to know it; that you are finding me, as you were always so good at doing. But I also think again about how the brain looks for patterns and for meaning. And I don't know. Is it coincidence? Just what happens when humans pay attention to what connects us?

But please know, if you can know: I am paying attention, doubting and perhaps resistant but also open. I know that I can't build a life around looking for you, listening for you. But I think that listening my way into the life that is waiting for me also includes listening for you, for how you might want to show up, even as you make your own way into whatever life is unfolding for you.

Oh, Sweetheart. It can seem a little silly, writing about things like shopping for a dress and shoes. But it is in the minutiae that I miss you most of all. I loved sharing the days with you, the moments that made up our life together. Loved living with you, loved moving through every day with you. Loved waking up to the smell of your coffee in the morning, curling up with you in your chair as we began our day. Loved climbing into bed with you at night and everything in between.

—Monday, June 16, 2014—

A quiet weekend, needing to rest and regather myself in the wake of last week.

Yesterday was Father's Day. I ached; for myself, and especially for Emile. His first Father's Day without you.

In the evening I finally gathered up the energy to go into the kitchen and make a lonely supper. Spaghetti. I turned on the TV, scrolled partway through the directory, and spotted a *Father Brown* mystery. You and I had watched one or two of those. I caught just the last twenty minutes or so as I worked in the kitchen.

What followed *Father Brown* was a UCF Artisode, one I had never seen before. It featured Theatre Downtown, and in the first minute of the show, when they were talking about the history of the theater, there was a still photo of five people. One of them was you.

Just this past Thursday I had been telling Christianne how good you were at finding me. How I would occasionally retreat to the bedroom if I was sad or bent out of shape, and at some point you would come looking for me. I've thought about that so often these past months: how you would find me, how I loved being found by you, how much I miss that.

These things that happen—the weird things with books, crossing paths with the woman at the bookshop, finding sparrows along the way, seeing you on TV on Father's Day—is this some intriguing but inherently meaningless pattern? Or is this you finding me?

—Friday, June 20, 2014—

The sensation lately that it was all something of a dream. You came into my life, seemingly out of the blue, and so quickly entered my heart. You left with nearly equal suddenness. Twelve years and one month we had: Halloween 2001 until the second day of Advent 2013.

What an innately liturgical fellow you were. *The cadenced liturgy of your life*, I wrote in the blessing for your service.

I could tell right away—I think even before I met you—that you were something other than I had ever encountered. You were always so much yourself, possessed of some inner core of strength and focus and giftedness, and a sense of wisdom and insight that you managed to wrest from what you had passed through.

That evening downtown at Guinevere's, at the open mic. I was hanging out in the gallery. You sat down beside me and said, *I hear you like Rumi.* (What a line!) And we picked up a conversation that seemed like it had been going on forever.

And another night, shortly after. I saw you across the room and was seized by the impulse—which I did not act on—to go over to you and say, *You know we're going to be married one day, right?* Uncharacteristically, I was not gripped by panic or the need to figure things out immediately. Trusted that if there was something between us to explore, it would unfold when the time was right.

Always some knowing about you. Knowing of you.

I saw you.

I said that to Christianne yesterday. That one of the best things we humans can do for each other, that perhaps the greatest gift we can give, is to see each other.

I saw you. And it was the easiest thing in the world. To be stunned by you and your remarkable gifts. To know you. To find myself known and seen.

Who am I, I said to Christianne yesterday, *when the person who saw and knew me best in all the world is gone from this world?*

Christianne and I have talked a good bit about my doubt and resistance to believing these synchronicities that keep happening are somehow an indication you abide and are interested in making yourself known. I've talked with her about how a couple of folks asked, early on, whether I sensed you with me and how painful the question became because I couldn't sense you except in memory. I've told her about how Raymond Carver keeps showing up, about sparrows, about your turning up on the kitchen TV on Father's Day. Have told her about how, in the midst of this but still somewhat distinct from it, there is a knowing that seems to be settling into my bones that has eased the anguish and, along with the synchronicities, has begun to erode my doubt and resistance.

But still, but still, I doubt and resist and question. What if these lovely synchronicities are simply and only that: a splendid network of coincidences, a constellation that doesn't have any inherent meaning or intent behind it? What if my noticing of these and my becoming open to them and looking and listening for them is merely a crutch, a coping mechanism for this part of my journey of grief?

And I can join with Maru in gently mocking myself. I can look at the seeming synchronicities that are piling up and wonder at how I can still doubt. But I still doubt, still resist, still wonder.

Christianne and I talked about this yesterday. She acknowledged that, yes, maybe the noticing and looking that I'm doing is a coping mechanism. *But what if it is?* she asked. *So what?*

She also said this: *You have a muscle in you that's keen, that's really well developed—that pays attention, that knows how to see things and put them together for us.* I was grateful for how she talked about that. It helped somehow, how she described it, and I wish I could remember it better, but I remember how it felt. Some kind of a doorway there. That maybe I'm not making up or imagining that there might be some intention, some meaning in these weird things that keep happening.

Christian Wiman, in *My Bright Abyss* (did you send him to me?):

> The task is not to "believe" in a life beyond this one; the task is to perceive it. Perception is not projection: we are not meant to project our experience of this life into another, nor are we meant to imagine, by means of the details of

this life (which is the only resource we have for imagining), some possible beyond. Life is not life without an afterlife, and there is no afterlife beyond the life we treasure and suffer and feel slipping from us moment by moment. I don't mean to hide within an impenetrable paradox. I mean to say something along the lines of what Paul Éluard said a century ago: "There is another world, but it is in this one." Or, more to the point, Christ two thousand years ago: "The kingdom of God is within you."

Perception versus projection. I've thought a lot about that. But even perception, when we are able to perceive rather than merely project, is only part of it. What meaning do we ascribe to what we perceive? What meaning do we discern?

I said this, too, to Christianne yesterday: I don't want to be a pathetic widow who can't let go. Who hangs on when she shouldn't. This connects back to my wondering if these things I'm noticing are just a coping mechanism that's normal to this phase of grief. Would believing that there's intention and meaning behind these synchronicities actually be an attempt to avoid reckoning with the awfulness of your absence?

I can say this, though: I don't feel stuck. I don't feel paralyzed. I'm doing the work. I'm trying to pay attention to what needs attention. I'm meeting with Christianne. I'm showing up here and laying down words on these pages. I'm talking and praying and trying to listen.

Christianne has talked with me about lingering. *Letting yourself be his beloved*, she put it one day, which prompted tears. I am coming to realize this may be the greater part of the invitation to me right now: to not be so concerned about getting stuck, about being a pathetic widow, about not being able to let go, but rather to allow myself to linger in this place where I know myself as your beloved. That it's okay to do this for now, and perhaps crucial to do this.

And talking also with Christianne about this yesterday: that perhaps my doubts have to do not so much with residual disbelief in the possibility that you abide but with some resistance to what it would mean to be in relationship with you now—as each of us is now, in our transformed states. I told Christianne about the retreat reflection I wrote for Easter Sunday about John's story of the meeting of Jesus and Mary Magdalene in the garden. Told her how this time around—the first Easter after your death—it came particularly clear to me that resurrection is not the same as return.

This is what I went on to write in that reflection:

You will learn, and soon, that it comes with a cost, that new life really means this: means new, means that it will not be the same as before, means that you cannot hold on to him, means that you will have to let go of everything in order to know him and love him as he is now. As *you* are now, yourself altered beyond imagining.

You will learn that the cost of resurrection is also the gift: that having to let go—*again*, but differently—will propel you into a life you could hardly have dreamed on your own. Into the aching and empty space of your outstretched arms will enter a whole new world.

This awful hollowing taking place in your chest: this is your heart becoming larger. This is the space you will need in order to hold him now.

I wrote those words about Jesus and Mary Magdalene and also, of course, about us. What does it mean to be in relationship with you now? How do I speak of relationship with you now? Is it possible to tend a relationship with you—to listen, to pay attention, to look for you—and also lean into whatever life is unfolding for me? Is being open to you part of how I find my new life?

What might it mean to be able to say not only *I saw you* but also *I see you*? Still. Now. Always.

On my walk today: thinking about how maybe I don't know everything there is to know about grief. (And being amused with myself that I should have thought I knew so much.) That maybe it's far more mysterious than I imagined; that, as awful as it is, it's shot through with more wonders than I dreamed.

Summer Solstice. A long day, for sure. I remember one of the nurses in the hospital saying, *The hours are long but the days are short.* Or maybe it was, *The days are long but the weeks are short.* Something like that. Time did such strange things in the hospital. Expanded and compressed all at the same time. And continues to do so. When we hit the six-month anniversary of your death, I was struck by how it felt so recent that you had died and an aching eternity at the same time.

Your absence continues to feel bizarre. Bewildering. Premature and abrupt and stupidly wrong. I don't think human brains are quite built to absorb this kind of loss. I'd like to think that this sensation—of how strange it feels that you are gone, how unreal (and all too real at the same time), which I can imagine is a pretty universal response to the death of the beloved—is some indication that you are not entirely gone, that it's not just my brain having a hard time adjusting to your absence.

Reading Raymond Carver led me to Tess Gallagher. I found a volume of her collected poetry at the library—*Midnight Lantern* (lovely title, lovely cover)—and was particularly moved by the poems from *Moon Crossing Bridge*, which she wrote after Ray's death. Ordered my own copy, and it has been such a good companion. I can't abide reading prose about grief, but poetry has been good medicine, and Tess's poems in particular. Like these:

Yes

Now we are like that flat cone of sand
in the garden of the Silver Pavilion in Kyōto
designed to appear only in moonlight.

Do you want me to mourn?
Do you want me to wear black?

Or like moonlight on whitest sand
to use your dark, to gleam, to shimmer?

I gleam.   I mourn.

After the Chinese

By daybreak a north wind has shaken
the snow from the fir boughs. No disguise
lasts long. Did you think there were no winds
under the earth? My Tartar horse prefers
a north wind. Did you think
a little time and death would stop me?
Didn't you choose me for the stubborn
set of my head, for green eyes that dared
the cheat and the haggler from our door?
I've worn a little path, an egg-shaped circle
around your grave keeping warm
while I talk to you. I'm the only one
in the graveyard. You chose well. No one
is as stubborn as me, and my Tartar horse
prefers a north wind.

I love the image of stubborn Tess beating an egg-shaped path
around Ray's grave. Love the question, *Did you think / a little time
and death would stop me?* Where I feel oppressed when I open books
about grief, reading a line like that opens a door. A world.

What might I need to be stubborn about right now?

On my walks before you died, when I would pray for you and for
us, my prayer often included these words: *Bless us in our marriage
and in our vocation, each and together.* I stopped praying that prayer
after you died. Lately the words have started coming back to me. I

am trying them on, trying to see what fits, praying with them, asking about them. Are we still married? I'm not sure. But are we wedded? Does that word fit? And do we still have a vocation together? Are there ways we can still work together, serve together, be in ministry together? And you—does your life now, if you have a life now, include living into your vocation in ways that never happened here?

I've been able to listen to some of your music lately. It was too hard for a long while. Could listen only to the bits and pieces involved in posting your Songmaker's Notebook pages for the online retreats. I did put together a closing video for the Lenten retreat that brought together all the images I created for the retreat and set them to "I Am With You Always." That involved listening to you sing the words *I am with you always* again and again and again. Which was awful and beautiful.

For months the only music of yours I could listen to was a recording from the early '80s of the song you wrote about the space shuttle—the *Columbia*—after the first time it went up. You and Jane performed it one night in Gainesville. She recorded it to cassette, then later transferred it to DAT and after that to MP3. Soon after you died, she sent it my way.

With the song having been recorded to cassette more than thirty years ago and going through multiple formats, I wasn't expecting much in the way of sound quality, but it was surprisingly good. Your voice was familiar but younger, and I think that helped me be able to hear it—that although I'd heard you sing it once, the song came from a time long before I knew you. It's a very cool song, and wonderful to have an audio artifact from that part of your life.

One day a couple or so weeks ago, I got out *One Man* and put it in the CD player. In some ways this has long been my favorite CD of yours. I like the unvarnished feel of it, recorded at a house concert just a month or so before we began dating. I remember when the concert happened—I missed it and must have been out of town. The first time we got together—one October evening at Barnes & Noble—you brought a copy of it with you. *These songs are some of who I am*, you wrote on the insert. *I hope you like them. G.*

I sure did like them. Still do. When I played the CD the other day for the first time since you died, I wept as I listened to the opening song—"The Unused Portion":

I've come to dedicate this unused portion
That I have been saving for so long
I cannot carry it
And I cannot put it down
And I can only seem to sing of it
In the lyrics of a song
I've come to dedicate this unused portion
That is not greatly in demand
I give it freely
Even though these many years
It's been such a part of who I am
And I have brought it here
To deliver into your hands

You wrote all those songs before I met you, but I cannot help but hear them now in the context of our relationship and from this side of your dying. Cannot help but hear this song as the one who was your audience, who was—and is—the glad and grateful recipient of the unused portion you offered, which was—and is—a treasure beyond anything I could have imagined.

I listened to all the CD except "Are We Abandoned." Could not make it through that one. Remember your talking about how it was inspired in large measure by seeing the movie *The Patriot*— the scene where Mel Gibson's character is going off to fight and is leaving his younger son, who weeps and begs him not to go, telling him he'll do anything if his father will stay. You sing:

I'll do anything
I'll say anything
Just don't leave me here alone

Yeah, not going to listen to that for a while. Have also listened to some of *Whenever I'm With You* and *This Man's Heart*. Have to take the listening in doses. It is heartbreaking to hear you, but I have been craving your voice.

I'm not sure when I'll be able to listen to your chapel songs: the songs you wrote for the Wellspring service, for that space that we shared together; the songs you shared in the spaces we created together in retreats and conferences and workshops across the country. The spaces that I loved creating together with you and can hardly imagine creating without you.

Tired, though I have done hardly anything all day. Slept in this morning. Went for a long walk at noontime (really need to start doing that earlier in the day). Despite the sleeping in, I gave in to a long nap this afternoon. Some reading. Some TV. This writing.

I have written my way into the dark on this longest day of the year. Hoping the words carry some light with them into this night. Aiming to be as stubborn as Tess and then some, persisting in writing, in asking, in praying, in looking and listening for whatever it is I need to see and hear and know. Beating a path around your life and mine until something gives, illumines, makes a way.

—SUNDAY, JUNE 22, 2014—

Made it to your great-niece's birthday party today and spent a good while talking with Greg, which both broke my heart and consoled it. As we talked, I was struck by how we are the two people in the world who have known you best. Somehow we got to talking about how artists sometimes struggle with being seen, with finding people who see them. Greg talked about how so many people, when they cross paths with someone creatively gifted, think of those gifts as a parlor trick, not understanding what goes into it, where it comes from, and what it means for the artist. And we acknowledged how you had hungered for this, to be seen and heard by people who recognized what you were about. Greg talked about how lonely it can be for an artist and how we can start to doubt ourselves and wonder if we're making all this up—the value of what we're doing, what we are trying to offer.

I am so grateful for Greg—that he saw you and heard you and got you and was in a position to come alongside you across the years with encouragement, prayer, conversation, and understanding (and love, always love), and also in wonderfully practical ways in the form of recording and producing your CDs. Holy cow. What would we have done without Greg?

I told Greg about how I've begun to listen to some of your songs again in the past couple of weeks and how moving it was to listen to the song "This Man's Heart," which you wrote for him out of your gladness and gratitude for his love and support. I am so glad for that song, that you created it as a gift of thanks to him:

> In this world
> In this world
> We all need someone
> To take our part
> And I stand here tonight before you
> By the love
> Of this man's heart

Thinking of those lyrics, I find myself thinking of that moment when you said, *The thing to remember here, Jan, is that I am on your side.* It was some years ago, on an occasion when I was dealing with a persistently difficult situation. We talked over options and possibilities, and then you said, *I am on your side.*

What incredibly powerful words to hear. And that is one of the most awful parts of not having you here, physically present: that I don't have you here to be on my side. I trust that if you abide, you are finding ways still to be on my side.

But still, but still, not to have that right at hand is an awful thing. I talked with Greg a little about that today, as we were talking about the rarity and the power of really being seen: how amazing it was to *live* with that kind of seeing, to have that from you on a daily basis, and now to be without it. And I think again of saying to Christianne the other day, *Who am I, now that the person who knew me best—who saw me best—is gone from this world?*

What an extraordinary gift to have had that for the time that I did. To have sensed that in you and received that from you from the beginning, even before we began dating. I remember mustering up the courage to read a couple of poems at Guinevere's one night—think it was the only time I ever did that. Not sure we had even had a conversation at that point—maybe just one—and you said something encouraging to me afterward. Something about how I needed to keep doing that.

Being seen by you has forever altered how I see myself. As bereft and alone as I feel, I feel the lingering impact of this and continue to see myself differently. Can imagine something of what you see, what you might say. And pray that somehow you still see me, are still knowing me.

So the Raymond Carver thing. I've written about the night I was having terrible insomnia in the first month or so after you died and suddenly felt compelled to get up and pull his book *All of Us* from the shelf. I wish I could remember when you gave it to me and if you said anything about why you had chosen to give me Raymond Carver. When did you first read him? What did he mean to you; what did you find in his words? But am grateful that you gave him to me, for whatever reason you did; what a comfort he has been, and Tess too. They keep popping up, especially Ray.

On the evening of June 2—the day that marked six months since you died—I was browsing your bookshelves and came across an issue of *Poetry* magazine from April 1989. I think that other than a few music-related magazines, this is the only magazine you own. I pulled it from the shelf—I hadn't seen it before—and there was Raymond Carver's photo on the cover. For Pete's sake. I wonder where you picked it up, and when.

On the cover, beneath his photo (in which he has a bit of a sly look on his face, almost as if meant for me—that he knew finding this magazine would come as a surprise and a gift), it says, *Raymond Carver: Last Poems*. The issue opens with four of his poems. They're all in *All of Us*, so I had read them before, but these two especially struck me on that particular night:

No Need

I see an empty place at the table.
Whose? Who else's? Who am I kidding?
The boat's waiting. No need for oars
or a wind. I've left the key
in the same place. You know where.
Remember me and all we did together.
Now, hold me tight. That's it. Kiss me
hard on the lips. There. Now
let me go, my dearest. Let me go.
We shall not meet again in this life,
so kiss me goodbye now. Here, kiss me again.
Now, my dearest, let me go.
It's time to be on the way.

Hummingbird
For Tess

Suppose I say *summer*,
write the word "hummingbird,"
put it in an envelope,
take it down the hill
to the box. When you open
my letter you will recall
those days and how much,
just how much, I love you.

Holy cow, just copying those out. Rips my heart open all over again. And the line about the key, much as you did with your keys just before we went to the hospital, leaving them in the bowl on top of your filing cabinet, your wedding band attached. Some time later, after you died, I removed the wedding band from your key ring, put it in the jewelry box on my dresser. An awful moment.

How extraordinary to come to know something of Ray in this time, to have his words accompanying me on this strange and awful and yet graced path. If it was you—if you were the one who sent him—thank you. Bless you.

And then the next day, coming across his book *Call If You Need Me* in the library.

I think Raymond Carver is stalking me, I said to Christianne. Or perhaps simply you, finding a way to find me. Thank you for Ray; thank you for Tess. For leading me to these two remarkable poets/ writers who found each other and whose love and grief and artistry were all bound together and are offering sustenance and solace in these days in ways that I can receive and absorb.

But oh, my goodness, Sweetheart. It all comes down to this, that I miss you so much I can hardly bear it. I've been thinking lately about how on one level, it doesn't matter what I do: I can take care of myself or not take care of myself, can attend to the grief or ignore the grief, can find ways to be creative with it or not, but none of it, nothing I do, can change that you are gone. I can pay attention to the ways you seem to be showing up, can find healthy ways to be open to that and take delight in that, but even that cannot alter the fact that you are not here in the flesh.

Futility was the word Christianne offered when I talked with her about this. Yes. It feels futile. I know it's important that I take care of myself and that I turn my attention where it's needed. But I feel so intensely helpless to do anything that will make a substantial difference in what my life looks like now. Without you. There is no changing that.

So what is yet possible? In the midst of your goneness, in the midst of how futile my actions seem, what is possible from here? For us? For me?

Much of what I'm dreaming and aiming toward has to do with things you and I were already planning, such as books and online retreats. Within this, what new dreams? And are there ways we can yet work together?

And you: What are you dreaming? Are there ways I can help you? I pray about this sometimes, when I pray for you. I pray that you will be released from every hindrance. That every bit of ill fortune will flee from you. That you will be set loose and know what it means to be truly free. That you will know how intensely and deeply and completely you are loved. I think taking care of myself is one way I can help you. And loving Emile is another way I can help you. But is there anything else? Is there anything I can do from this side of the veil?

Wanting to *do*. Wanting to have something tangible and tactile, something real—this keeps coming up in my grieving. I imagine it's a normal part of grieving, wanting to be able to do something that will be helpful to you, to Emile, to me. To have something besides this awful sense of helplessness and futility.

Please. If there's something I can do to be helpful, let me know. I am listening.

I see you.

—Monday, June 23, 2014—

Ospreys have been in the neighborhood this week, wheeling and crying. I keep thinking of your song "The Osprey Circles." How you sang about that bird that inhabits two worlds, air and water; how it abandons the sky to propel itself toward the water, seeking its prize, its heart's desire:

O let me be that bird of two worlds
In the blinding blue
To dive into the mirror of the lake
As I was meant to do

Praying this for you. That you have propelled yourself—or at least released yourself—with abandon toward where you need to be. I pray this, not even knowing quite what it means. But praying that you are knowing what it is to soar and to arrive.

And I think of this: How I would tell you, *You are my true love.* And you would respond, *You are my heart's desire.* Think you were the one who first began this, who gave these words to me. How often we said them.

The first time you told me you loved me. You touched my face and said, *Do you know I am deeply in love with you?* And I said, *I do now.* And I told you I loved you, had already been loving you; told you that I had found myself wondering, *What's that thing you say when you love someone but it feels too soon to say I love you?* But you said it, and it wasn't too soon.

You always had great timing. Except at the end, it seems. Though after you died, maybe in the first month or so, I found myself thinking, *If I can trust that he entered my life with such perfect timing, can I trust the timing of his leaving?* The thought doesn't help all that much, but it felt like an important wondering.

A long walk this morning. The walking helps. Trying to do it nearly every day. Something about being in motion. Think it helps me absorb what's unfolding. Finding some kind of rhythm in it.

Have been noticing hawks, too, on my walks, along with the ospreys. Was in the front room this morning and saw a hawk land on the porch. Hadn't seen one come that close before.

Oh, my talented, handsome, beautiful husband. How do people survive this kind of loss? How am I supposed to? A breath at a time, I know. But the breath keeps getting knocked from me.

Let me be that bird of two worlds.

—Tuesday, June 24, 2014—

Rain! I was maybe two minutes into a lovely evening walk when it began. I had thought the rain was over. But, like grief, it has a way of surprising me.

So I am sitting on the front porch, where I have been spending a lot of time in the past few months. Lovely evening light. Watching the rain come down and hearing thunder in the distance. Most often, when I'm writing to you, I'm on the porch. Remembering conversations we used to have out here. We would talk about the house and the possibility of buying it. Would talk about where we'd like to live, what kind of home we would like to have. Would talk about our life together, about possibilities and dreams.

The extra chair on the porch feels very lonely. Empty.

Do you dream still? Do you have imaginings about how your life will unfold from here, from where you are now? What choices and possibilities do you have? Do you dream about how my life will unfold? From where you are, are you able to see things I can't see right now? Can you work to inspire me in any particular directions?

I remember a walk we took very early in our relationship. I was over at your house one night, and we set out into the dark. It was a misty night, and very still. We didn't see anybody. It felt like another world, or this world but another dimension. Mysterious and enchanted. Looking at the houses we passed, we began to talk about what we liked in houses, the kind of houses we felt drawn to and imagined living in. When we got back to your house, we lingered outside for a bit. You turned to me and said, *One thing I know is, whatever kind of house I imagine living in, you're in it.*

And how wonderful that was to hear. To know, even then, so early. That my home was with you.

Had lunch with Karen today.

I said to her, *Here's the kind of thing that runs through my head: What if Gary finds someone in heaven? What if he falls in love with someone there?*

That's the kind of question I sometimes find visiting me. It seems irrational on one hand, but why not? If you do abide, if somehow we'll see each other again, what then? What if you've taken up with someone else by then? It never occurred to me until recently that such a possibility might exist.

Talked also with Karen, practically in the same breath, about how I sense that part of my work is to be the person who can hold the pieces of your life, the life you had here; that this includes things like being the person who archives your work and goes through your pictures and knows your story. And talked with her about what a remarkable thing it is, what a gift, that I should be the person who gets to do this; that I am the person in all the world who knows Gary Doles the best. How astounding is that? At the same time, feeling anxious about what lies ahead—what I might lose and have to let go of.

I've talked with Christianne about trying to let go of anticipatory grief, how that's some of the worst grief. I'm trying not to get ahead of myself. I'm trying to trust that in each step, I'll know what I need and have what I need. And that perhaps it won't be as awful as I imagine from this vantage point. Challenging to trust the unfolding.

Thinking, too, about a conversation I had with Christianne in the past week or two. I told her about reading Carver's poem "For Tess" and how, weeping, I began to write this:

It Is Hard Being Wedded to the Dead

It is hard
being wedded
to the dead;
they make different claims,
offer comforts
that do not feel comfortable
at the first.

They do not let you
remain numb.
Neither do they allow you
to languish forever
in your grief.

They will safeguard
your sorrow
but will not permit

that it should become
your new country,
your home.

They knew you first
in joy,
in delight,
and though they will be patient
when you travel
by other roads,
it is here
that they will wait
for you,
here they can best
be found

where the river runs deep
with gladness,
the water over each stone
singing your
unforgotten name.

Christianne and I found ourselves focusing especially on the
last line, about the river whose water sings, over each stone, *your
unforgotten name.* I talked with her about how things surface in my
poetry that would be hard to get to otherwise and how that line was
one of those occasions: that I need to know, want to know, that you
haven't forgotten me.

I talked with Christianne about my wonderings about the afterlife, if there is an afterlife. Are you allowed to remember those
you loved? Namely, me? Or does leaning into your life now require
forgetting what has gone before, require not knowing and not being able to stay connected to us, to me?

That poem—that line—came as solace unbidden, offering
some measure of reassurance that I am not forgotten by you, that I
am remembered and loved. And, I pray, known even now.

PART TWO
Learning the Language

Sparrow Says

Who told you
this would be
so final,
so complete?

Be at peace.
It will not be
so endless
as that.

Feels like a wall,
yes.
Feels like a door
never stops closing,
yes.

But listen.
We have ways
and ways.

Praying last night. Struggling with how to pray for you, how to pray with you. Feeling like I had hit a wall. And made that part of the prayer, telling God, *I have hit a wall, and I don't know what to do; I don't know how to pray.*

Immediately—just like that—an image came to me from a story that Clarissa Pinkola Estés told at the Women's Convocation. I can't remember much of the story, but it involved a wall that had been filled and wounded with nails. The people pulled the nails from the wall, but the restoration of the wall did not end there. Someone said, *We can put seeds in the wounds.*

I remembered that story because just a few days ago, I came across a small scrap of paper on the island in your studio. I don't remember why I was in there and why I picked up this particular piece of paper on this day, but on the scrap, as we listened to Clarissa speak, you had written this: *Nails in the wall story—seeds in the wounds—the story's not over.*

I remember how we were both so taken with her story of the wall and the seeds.

The image felt like a gift from you. When I remembered the image and the scrap of paper with those words you had written, I went and got it, read it again, and wept with the sorrow and the beauty and the wonder of it, that those words should reach me at that time, in that way.

I don't know what it would mean, what it would look like, what it would involve, to put seeds in this wall that I've hit. But it feels like a place of prayer, a place to begin, a place to linger. I imagine you on the other side of that wall, putting seeds in from that side, and that somehow we are creating a story together. Still.

The other day, on an index card, I wrote these words: *You who loved stories—how you have now become all story.*

Part of what last night gave me is the sense that the story isn't finished. Is it something we can work on together?

—Saturday, June 28, 2014—

On my walk this morning, I found myself thinking about how hard it sometimes seems to sense you, how I would like to have a clearer sense of you and who you are now. And these words came to the surface: *You don't have to make it so hard. And you don't have to be so sad.* I thought of how, early on, when people asked if I sensed you with me, I said, *What if I reach out, and he isn't there?* And today I sensed something that felt like you saying, *You don't even have to reach. All you need to do is receive.*

I don't know if that's you or if I'm projecting. Maybe it doesn't matter. I recognize the truth that those words contain, at least with respect to not making it so hard, that I don't have to reach. I can't promise not to be so sad. But I'm intrigued by the thought of receiving rather than reaching.

Receive is a word that's recently come up for me, joining earlier words such as *listen* and *ask*. And also the phrase *You must be very still*, feeling as if it, in particular, had come from you: that at this point in the journey, sensing you is connected to stillness and to the silence I've been craving, especially at night in my time of prayer and quiet and reading and listening. I talked briefly with Christianne this week about those nighttime practices and how, although I don't typically feel you *with* me in a particularly present kind of way—not in an eerie, sensing-you-at-my-shoulder fashion—entering that space and that practice of listening and being open helps me be receptive to those times when you do seem to be stirring, like in the Raymond Carver books.

As I often tell Christianne (too often, perhaps, as if I want to make sure she knows I'm not going off the deep end), I'm aware there may be no inherent meaning in the synchronicities and intriguing oddities that occur. The deepening sense I have in my bones that you abide, that you persist, may be nothing more than projection. But still it feels like something to pay attention to. In healthy ways, as I make sure to tell Christianne. And seem to feel it's important to say to you.

Yes. Keenly aware that I often work harder at things than I

need to. Especially with this. But how not to, with this?

And maybe that's a place of prayer. And maybe that's part of the resting I'm doing now. Trying not to work so hard. And understanding that resting is part of the work I need to do now.

A couple of miscellaneous things to capture.

One: Recently came across a few index cards with notes I'd scribbled from a talk given by Mary Stamps and Sister Mary Reuter at the Saint Brigid's retreat last summer. These notes were from Sister Mary Reuter's talk: *Here and now is where we meet and respond to God. In situations of instability, look for the possibilities. A time to develop qualities—vulnerability, etc. Asking for help and also developing our inner resources.* Felt apt for where I am now. Looking for possibilities. Discerning what might help me and who can provide that help. Summoning interior strength while at the same time recognizing the places where I'm vulnerable and need to ask for help or pray for protection so that my vulnerability doesn't become perilous.

Another miscellaneous bit: Several nights ago, I dreamed of being in Seattle. I was walking through a neighborhood, on my way to meet you somewhere in the city. I found myself doubling back in the neighborhood, lost, passing through a restaurant or some place I had already walked through before. I kept walking and walking. Then, at a high spot in the city, I could see the water, and I knew which way to go—that if I walked toward the water, I would find you.

My dreaming life has seemed odd since you died. I don't remember many of my dreams, and of the ones I do remember, many of them seem silly, stupid, inconsequential. Early on I figured it had to do at least in part with the disruption in my sleeping patterns after you died, that maybe my sleeping issues were disrupting my dreams as well. My sleep patterns are improving, though still not great, and still it feels like my dream life is—I don't know, *stupid* is the word that keeps coming to mind. It's a matter of prayer for me;

every night, I ask you to be in my dreaming, to meet me there, to bring me dreams of comfort and insight. I'm not overly concerned about the dreaming (or not dreaming or having stupid dreams). Simply a noticing of something that has begun to feel odd, as it's extended more than seven months now.

It did occur to me some months ago that perhaps it was a mercy I'm not remembering many of my dreams in the wake of your death, that perhaps they're disturbing, though it seems I would remember disturbing ones.

Though I haven't dreamed often of you (that I can remember) since you died, I'm always grateful for the times you show up. Like in the dream that came maybe a couple of months ago. We were sitting here in our comfy chairs—where I'm sitting now, having abandoned the porch to the mosquitoes. You were back, and alive; your dying had been a terrible mistake but had been fixed and put right. You were pretty nonchalant about it; it seemed normal to you to be here. I was overwhelmed with joy and was trying to find words to convey how much I had missed you and what a marvel it was that you were back.

Sweetheart. My brain still can't fathom it, not having you here in the flesh. Not being able to hear your voice, your ready laughter. Not being able to touch you. Not being held in your gaze. I am praying that something in these words will reach you. That they will find their way into the thin place between us. That they will be part of what thins the veil between us. That they, and the longing that infuses them and gives rise to them, will come to you as a blessing and a gift: you who were, and are, an astounding blessing and gift to me. *My true love, my heart's desire.*

—SATURDAY, JULY 5, 2014—
Gainesville, Florida

A quiet night in Gainesville. Crickets humming in Mom and Dad's back yard. The fan turning. The ticking of your watch.

I wear that watch sometimes these days, though it vexed me

when you were alive. How loudly it ticked. I would sometimes move it to another room so I couldn't hear it. You liked the ticking, found it soothing, were perplexed why it disturbed me.

When I went to Toronto in April, I grabbed your watch on impulse as I was leaving the house. Began to wear it some. Told Sally one day how I had disliked its loud ticking. *Now I think it sounds like a heartbeat*, I said to her.

—Sunday, July 6, 2014—
Gainesville

Grateful for the space of respite here in Gainesville, the change of scenery. Being away from home—our home—doesn't make me ache any less, but it helps to be in a different place and with people, helps me hold the ache a little differently and not absorb the full force of it all alone.

And you—do you ache? Or does being where you are free you from aching? Is that part of the point of being where you are, wherever that is? I have worried about you, fearful about what it was like for you to find yourself beyond this life, particularly with regard to Emile—how brokenhearted I thought you would be not to be here for him in the ways you had planned. I have not entirely given up those fears and concerns but am praying that somehow this works out, to whatever extent it possibly can; that Emile will somehow know you; that you will be able to help him from where you are.

I find myself wondering this night: Are there any questions you live with? Or does being where you are give you a knowing that frees you from questions? It's strange to ponder. Questions are such a fundamental part of who I am, how I think and pray and move through the world. Questions have been such a part of who we have been together. You have been such a marvelous question-asker. Two early ones I remember you asking: *Have you ever had your heart broken?* and *When has somebody given you a gift that made you feel known?* Especially liked that one. And how good you were at doing that very thing: giving me gifts that made me feel known.

I miss your questions. Miss the way you were so brilliant at knowing what to ask. Miss how you helped me identify the questions and hold them and live with them. Miss how I could call out from my studio or walk down the hall to your studio and ask you a question. What am I supposed to do with my questions now? Is there still a place within the questions where you can meet me? I have so many of them now. More than ever.

—Thursday, July 10, 2014—
Toronto

You have sparrows in Belfast. Did you know that? An email from Jenny arrived just as I was about to leave the house to walk down to the café. Jenny was on the Lenten retreat and became such a lovely part of the community. She posted images of several sparrows and has continued to send me lovely emails with photos of sparrows and thin places. On Pentecost Day, she sent a note that included these words:

> I am praying so much for you. There are sparrows on the feeder (albeit not easy to see in the photograph), and the bog is green after the winter brown. Lots of people out cutting it, and it's full of little stacks drying in the sun.

Pentecost was a difficult day, so full of missing you, and it was a gift to receive her photo and words about sparrows on the bog.

Today she sent a couple of emails that included some enchanting photos of thin places, along with these words:

> We have been helping my mother, who is 92, in her wonderful garden and feeding crumbs to Gary's sparrows. They loved the crumbs but were too shy to be photographed and flew away to safety when I approached with a camera, so you have to see them in your dreaming.
> I will be praying for your time in Toronto and your

book of blessings, and the picture came into my mind of the woman who blessed Jesus by washing his feet with her tears, and I pray that amidst the heartbreak of your labyrinth of grief you will yourself find a place and a still moment where you are blessed.

And it's good to hear of your dream to come to this part of the world and visit Gary's Faddan More bog and so much else. When that time comes you are welcome to spend a while in our little cottage in Donegal between mountains and bog and sea, where the sparrows sing.

So you have sparrows in Belfast, Sweetheart, and an Irish bog. I love it and am grateful for Jenny's kindness.

—TUESDAY, JULY 15, 2014—
Toronto

I've had archiving your work very much on my mind of late. Have thought about it often since shortly after your death but hadn't been ready (or quite known how) to deal with it in an organized fashion: your papers, DVDs, VHS tapes, audiocassettes, everything. But it's feeling more pressing, particularly to make sure I have your cassettes and VHS tapes transferred and backed up.

The night before I went up to Gainesville for the Fourth of July weekend, I called Mom and Dad. In our conversation I shared with them that I was experiencing some pre-trip anxiety as I prepared to leave for Canada and that my anxiety was particularly focused on your stuff; I was uneasy about leaving all those tapes and cassettes and photographs and much of your written work at the house, unattended, for three weeks. I was already planning to take your Martin guitars up to Mom and Dad's for safekeeping while I was away. But I had questions about the other stuff, including some boxes of your writing that included handwritten song lyrics going back perhaps thirty years. I decided to ask Mom and Dad for their counsel instead of merely chasing the questions around in my head.

It helped. They told me to bring whatever I wanted and leave it at the house while I was away. Just talking about it with them brought clarity and relief.

I spent several hours that night going through your studio, deciding what to bring. Challenging—not so much deciding what to gather up but going through your things in the first place. It still feels so wrong that you are gone and that I am needing to do this kind of work with the tangible pieces you left behind—this body of work, these things that are left of your life. Toward the end I started feeling suffocated—a bit like the day you died (though not as severe), when at one point, standing beside your bed, I suddenly felt suffocated and sensed it was because you—your spirit, your soul—was no longer there, inside your body. Prior to that, I had wanted to spend as much time as possible in your room (while minding the hospital staff, who told me it was important not to spend all my time there) to be present to you, to be with you. But on that last day, when that feeling of suffocation suddenly began to set in, I realized something had shifted in both of us, and I needed to step out for a bit.

The night I was going through your things, before leaving for Gainesville, I think the stifling sensation was largely because I had been at the sorting for a while and was needing to stop. I pushed through for a few more minutes, until I'd gathered most everything I wanted to take. I got a bit of rest—it took a long time to finally fall asleep after all that—and then, the next morning, I loaded up your Martins and the boxes of your writings and cassettes and VHS tapes and DVDs and CDs and photographs and headed for Gainesville. Once I'd unloaded everything in my room there, it felt strange to see the bulk of your work gathered together like that, in one place (that wasn't our home). As if this was what was left of your life, stacked up on the spare bed. But also a relief to leave it in Mom and Dad's hands.

I do know that those things are not all that's left of your life, that the best of you—the uncountable, stunning, enduring wealth of you—is carried on in me and in Emile and in others who love you. But I do want to do the best I can to preserve and tend the treasures you have left behind, bizarre though it so often feels that I am in this position, so much sooner than either of us anticipated. I remember again how you would sometimes say, *Tomorrow is promised to no man.* I always thought it was a quote from someone, but in searching for it just now, I can't find the original source; it seems to be one of those phrases that people quote as being from the Bible but isn't actually in there, at least not in quite those words.

The day before I left for Toronto, in the midst of the packing and tidying, my eyes fell on the bowl on the table by your side of our bed, the bowl you had, night by night, filled with the wrappers from your Breathe Right strips. It was really full! Couldn't even guess how many were in there. I picked up the bowl and went to the trash can in the kitchen. Opened the lid. And hesitated to throw them away. They were evidence of you and part of your nightly ritual. How many nights you lay beside me and, after we had read and talked and laughed, you unwrapped one of those Breathe Right strips, put the strip on your nose, and tossed the wrapper in that bowl.

Hesitating at the trash can, I thought again about saving the strips and creating something artful from them. Thought about calling Peg and asking for her counsel. Could not imagine what I would do with them, what I might create from them. And because I couldn't imagine, I finally scooped my hand into the bowl, pulled out a fistful of the strips, and let them fall into the trash. Did this again and again until the bowl was empty, save for the index card you had put in there long ago. *I love you*, I had written on the card. Had probably placed it on your pillow at the time. I left the card in the bowl, then put the bowl back on your table beside the bed that was ours.

For all those nights we lay beside each other in our bed, gathering up the threads of the day; for all we shared in that bed; for every time you closed your book, turned out the light on your bedside table, enfolded me and told me you loved me and sent me into the night with kisses: Thank you. Bless you. If there is night where you are, may you have a good night. May you know the love that enfolds you this night and in every moment. *Sweet dreams, Sweetheart. I love you.*

—Wednesday, July 16, 2014—
Toronto

It is a beautiful morning. Lots of clouds but also sun peeking through. I'm sitting at the kitchen table with the sliding glass doors open. Listening to birds—sparrows? I've seen lots of them around here—and the traffic beyond.

I brought Tess Gallagher's book *Moon Crossing Bridge* up here with me. It has been a remarkable companion on this journey. Was rereading this one last night:

Valentine Delivered by a Raven

Its beak is red and it has a battlefield-look,
as if it's had its pickings and come away
of its own volition. Elsewhere the Emperor Frederick
sleeps on, guarded by ravens, and may yet rise
from deathly slumber and walk the earth.
Who knows what's long enough
when death's involved. I stand on my love's grave
and say aloud in a swoop of gulls over
the bay, "I kiss your lips, babe," and it's not
grotesque, even though the mind knows what it
knows, and mostly doesn't. Language,
that great concealer, is more than generous, gives
always what it doesn't have. I stare into the dazzling
impertinent eye of the messenger. He's
been tending the dead so long his eyes are garnets,
his wings cracked open to either side, two
fissures savage with light. I bend
in recognition and take up a holly bough left

as in the old adornment of doorways. The hard, red
berries glisten and tremble in their nest of
green, so when he speaks I hear him
with the attention of a red berry before a covetous
bright eye, and what I need I take
in empires before he flaps away on my love's errands
and I am cinnabar and fog in the doorway.

Who knows what's long enough / when death's involved. Yes. I am
so aware of my fatigue and inertia as I sit here. I have ideas about
the projects I want to be working on, things I brought with me to
work on, and I feel the tug and press of them. And I do feel energy
around them; they're things I want to be working on, projects that
tickle my imagination. But when it comes right down to it, when
it comes to figuring out how to organize my life and the rhythm of
my days in order to work on them, I feel overwhelmed.

In the midst of this are my questions about how I tend my
grief and how present to be to it. Particularly in this initial year of
your being gone (*gone*; I have these moments where I am horrified
all over again at the unfathomable reality of that, of how gone you
are from this life), it feels important to attend well to the grief,
to do this writing, to do the work with Christianne, to let myself
linger, as she says, in being your beloved. And, again, I feel the
need to qualify that the lingering is (I hope) not about grasping or
wallowing or letting myself remain stuck. Attending to the grief,
lingering in this extraordinary love, feeling the full measure of what
it meant to be your beloved, and discerning what it means still—it
feels important and necessary and part of what it means to find my
way into the life that is unfolding in front of me.

But how to hold the two together? How to attend to the grief
and also work on these other projects when my energy already feels
so limited? And how do I cultivate my energy? Just this week I've
started making it a specific matter of prayer, asking that I will know
what God is calling me to do right now, where to give myself, and
that I will be given the energy I need to do it.

A crying bout just now as I grapple with these questions and with the sorrow that ebbs and flows in its intensity but is always there, flowing beneath every moment of every day. I can feel the struggle raging within me around these questions of how to be present to the grief—how much energy do I give it?—and how to discern what else I'm meant to do right now. Amidst the tears, I sat myself down beside Sammy-the-dog in the hall. At first he mostly ignored me while I wept. Then he stood up and got really close as I petted him for a bit. Then he grabbed one of my tear-soaked tissues in his mouth, ran under the table, and ate it. As if, perhaps, he thought it was time for me to stop crying.

I suspect the tears were prompted in part by my struggle this morning to know where best to direct what energy I have for writing—how and where to steward it. I'm hoping the writing I'm doing here in these pages will help. That in addition to the primary reasons I'm doing this—among them, to gather your story and our stories; to help me wade through my grief; to have a place where I feel connected to you, so that the grief itself doesn't become my primary tether to you—the act of writing itself will establish a rhythm of creating and will help inspire other writing. I'm looking for a different phrase than *prime the pump*, but that's the gist of it. Praying that this practice—both the rhythm and the content of it—will help me establish other practices of writing.

It makes me think of our first phone conversation. Somehow we began talking about practices, and I shared those lines from a Rumi poem that I've so often used, from "The Sunrise Ruby":

Work. Keep digging your well.
Don't think about getting off from work.
Water is there somewhere.

Submit to a daily practice.
Your loyalty to that
is a ring on the door.

Keep knocking, and the joy inside
will eventually open a window
and look out to see who's there.

Have always been drawn to those lines for the wonderful image
they provide of what it means to practice, to have a discipline—
that it's not about drudgery but about giving ourselves to an action
again and again over time in order to find the joy and life it holds
for us, the joy and life that can be found only when we engage the
practice over time. I don't remember much of what we said except
that you got it, knew what it meant to practice in that way. Think
you talked some about tae kwon do, which you studied for many
years and in which you earned a black belt.

Where do I need to be digging and knocking now? What do I
need to be practicing now? I know some of the answers but not all.
More questions for prayer. A practice in itself. More than one practice—discerning the questions in the first place, then remembering
to pray about them. And to listen.

This morning, as I woke, I realized I had your song "Raise This
Hour" going through my head. A lovely song for beginning the day:

Raise this hour into the arms of heaven
Let the gates of time be opened wide
Raise this hour into your holy presence
Lift us on unmeasurable tides

In this universe of moments
Every moment one by one
In this universe of moments
Let this moment be eternity

A thousand years
Doesn't mean a thing to you

How many stars are in the sky
How many of your children always in your eye

Even the sparrow finds a home
And we will find...

Until listening to part of the song just now, I had momentarily forgotten there's a sparrow in this song, finding its way home. Grateful for that.

—Thursday, July 17, 2014—
Toronto

Who knows what's long enough / when death's involved. To spiral back around to that for a moment. At the heart of my pondering and writing yesterday are these questions around time and grief: How much energy do I give to the grief? How long do I give it such primary focus? I know that I have only so much control when it comes to the grief; to a large extent, the grief will decide when it's time to shift in certain directions. But I do have discernment when it comes to things such as how much intentional focus I bring to it; for instance, how much time I give to writing these pages here and how I craft the rhythm of my days. And that's one of the big questions I'm chewing on right now: Just how do I craft the rhythm of my days, especially when my energy feels so limited?

I think the invitation to me right now is twofold: to do what lies in my power to get the rest and sleep I need; and, when I'm tired, to hold my fatigue more loosely (as you once counseled)—to pray for the energy I need and to discern where there are pockets or wellsprings of energy within me. I imagine it's a given, in this time of grieving, that I'm going to be tired for a long time. But it feels important to begin to challenge myself around this, to take some small steps to summon more energy and focus. And to continue to pray to know where to turn my attention and to ask for the energy I need.

Susan LaBarr wrote today regarding a blessing of mine she's set to music. A publishing house wants to publish the composition and has sent me a contract. I emailed her this morning with a couple of questions and asked for a recording of the song. Received an email back from her with a link to a video of the Missouri State Concert Chorale performing it in honor of the conductor, who was retiring after thirty-five years of teaching at MSU; Susan composed the piece especially for him. It's a beautiful piece and made me quite weepy. This is the blessing:

In the leaving,
in the letting go,
let there be this
to hold onto
at the last:

the enduring of love,
the persisting of hope,
the remembering of joy,

the offering of gratitude,
the receiving of grace,
the blessing of peace.

I wrote it two years ago for Ascension Sunday. In writing back to Susan, I talked about how many of my words have taken on different shades of meaning on this side of your dying. Shared "God of the Living" with her as an example. Still gives me the willies— that I wrote that just nine days before you went into the hospital, with no thought of our situation or of how much I would need the blessing for myself, and how soon:

GOD OF THE LIVING

When the wall
between the worlds

is too firm,
too close.

When it seems
all solidity
and sharp edges.

When every morning
you wake as if
flattened against it,
its forbidding presence
fairly pressing the breath
from you
all over again.

Then may you be given
a glimpse
of how weak the wall

and how strong what stirs
on the other side,

breathing with you
and blessing you
still,
forever bound to you
but freeing you
into this living,
into this world
so much wider
than you ever knew.

Other than "Blessing for One Already Brave," this was the
last blessing I worked on before your death, the last one you ever
saw and helped me with. I have thought of it often in these past
months, along with the lectionary reading that inspired it, shortly after All Saints' Day: the one where Jesus, in response to the

religious leaders' question about levirate marriage and the afterlife, says to them, *Now he is God not of the dead, but of the living; for to him all of them are alive* (Luke 20:38). That's radical—that, according to Jesus, God makes no distinction between the dead and the living. What does that mean for us Christians? What does that mean for *us*, you and me?

Clearly there's a distinction on this side of the veil. This is part of what I wrote to preface the blessing:

> On this side of the veil, we feel the distinction keenly, and Jesus does not dismiss or disparage this. Bent as he is on breaking down the walls of division, however, he cannot resist pressing against this one, the wall we perceive between the living and the dead. With his own death and resurrection almost upon him, Jesus pushes against that wall, shows it for what it is, challenges us to enter anew into our living and into our world that is so much larger, so much more mysterious than we dreamed.

But, again, what does this mean for those of us who live on this side of the veil? What does this mean for you and me?

—Friday, July 18, 2014—
Toronto

Hadn't been much out of the house for a couple of days, other than to take walks, so thought I would stir myself to at least get out this morning. I got up soon after nine, and still, somehow, with one thing and another—including letting Sammy out for a bit—I didn't manage to leave the house until about eleven. I would be hard pressed to say just how the time disappeared, since, except when I was sitting down for breakfast for a few minutes, I was in motion the whole time.

Having gotten myself to this café, I think of Brenda saying to me, early on, something about how there would be days when just

getting out of bed and dressing myself would be worth a *Ta da!*
There have been occasions when I've managed not only to do that
(think I've managed to do that every day!) but to actually make
myself presentable to go out into the world, and I've paused at the
door on my way out and said, in honor of Brenda (and myself),
Ta da!

I'm still pondering that passage from Luke that I wrote about
yesterday. It makes me think of some words Tess uses as an epigraph
to the second section of *Moon Crossing Bridge*; they come from a
letter from Jeff Keller:

> If we believe in the soul, then perhaps we have more in com-
> mon with the dead than the living.

In my praying last night, I thought again of how I had a sense
of you wanting me to know that feeling connected with you doesn't
require me to reach out for it, that what I need to do is simply receive. I wanted to feel that connection in more than memory and
didn't feel it. What does this mean? I did find myself also thinking
that perhaps trying to sense an awareness of you is something like
a fish trying to become aware of the water, that perhaps the truth
is that you are so present to me that it's hard for me to notice it in
a specific way.

I can't help but wonder if what I'm trying to do here in these
pages is futile. But I keep coming back to the thought that whatever
it is I'm doing here—continuing to show up, continuing to write,
continuing to ask the necessary questions, continuing to wrestle—
is important. That it's not a place of being stuck or refusing to move
forward but that it's somehow part of how I'm listening for the life
that is unfolding from here. Whatever that looks like.

I think Jeff Keller's words in Tess's book mean, in part, that
the soul is our place of connection, that it is what abides beyond
this life. If that's true, then it's also true that the soul is our place of
connection, resonance, kinship. And that what flows through our
souls, what actively connects us, is love.

This makes me think of a comment that Janet Horman offered

in response to the wedding photo I posted on what would have been our fourth anniversary. She wrote, *What a beautiful picture, Jan. Four years was way too short. With gratitude, I know that love is not bound or diminished by death, but instead love bridges the divide. May God be with both of you.*

Thought that was beautiful. I love that image of love bridging the divide. Even as you feel so horribly, terribly gone, I have a deepening sensation that you are still somehow present in ways that are difficult to describe and that whatever connection is there, it is fueled and made possible by love; that in this strange country I have entered, love is the bridge.

There's something about the image of *this strange country I have entered*—something perhaps to explore. I remember commenting to someone soon after you died that I had just gotten a passport to a country I had hoped not to enter anytime soon. Awful terrain. No map. No visible path. Having to carve a path for myself, one that still manages to have such difficult twistings and turnings. And still, along the way, wellsprings to be found. Secret rooms offering hospitality and rest and blessing. No one to make the path for me—not what I would want anyway—but occasional signs and markers left for me to find. Like Tess's poetry. And Ray's. Christianne coming alongside. And you—catching hints and glimpses of you, or at least of how you might be stirring.

With Christianne two or three weeks ago, talking about these *receivings* (as she put it) that sometimes happen, I told her that I have some sense of you as a verb but not as a noun; that I see what might be signs of your activity in my life, but I'm not sure who you are now. But, as I told her, maybe who you are for me right now is someone who stirs in these ways and it's not for me to know more of you than this right now. Still, one wants a glimpse. *Show me your face*, I often pray.

Back to Janet's comment about how love bridges the divide. Bridges have come up a few times these past months. Oh! I haven't written about the best bridge that's shown up. From Hafiz:

A Crystal Rim

The
Earth
Lifts its glass to the sun
And light—light
Is poured.

A bird
Comes and sits on a crystal rim
And from my forest cave I
Hear singing,

So I run to the edge of existence
And join my soul in love.

I lift my heart to God
And grace is poured.

An emerald bird rises from inside me
And now sits
Upon the Beloved's
Glass.

I have left that dark cave forever.
My body has blended with His.

I lay my wing
As a bridge to you

So that you can join us
Singing.

Some years back I gave you a copy of Daniel Ladinsky's collection of poems by Hafiz, *The Gift*. You left a bookmark—a ticket from one of our visits to Disney—and the place where you left that bookmark is the spread that includes this poem.

I was tremendously struck by Hafiz's words, *I lay my wing / As a bridge to you / So that you can join us / Singing.* The image of the wing as a bridge—such a beautiful new image for me. Could do a whole *lectio* session just on that. And perhaps should. I'm hearing the poem as if said in your voice. Thinking of how you seem to be stirring in birds as well as books. How might wings be a bridge for me, for us?

One day at Borders in Winter Park—the Borders where we first met—you and I were browsing, and I came across a very big book about birds. It had such beautiful historical plates. You bought the book for me, and you inscribed it: *For the girl who loved birds and became the woman I love.*

Love that inscription.

Birds. There are so many sparrows up here. Outside with Sammy this morning, I saw (and heard) so many of them flitting among the hedges. Jenny sent me another sparrow a few days ago. *If you look carefully underneath the green hose in the middle of the photo*, she wrote, *you hopefully can see Gary's little brown sparrow that enjoyed the crumbs we left out.*

Thinking of how birds navigate the space between earth and sky. Between the world and the heavens. And how I can sometimes become bound in patterns of thought and fixed ideas. Sensing an invitation to attend to imagination—as the language of the soul, as a place of meeting, as a practice that is crucial to finding the path ahead. A path that might require wings, might ask for ways of moving and being in the world that are more risky, more trusting, more beautifully daring.

The morning I left to fly up here, I turned on the TV for a few minutes during breakfast. Came across a show that you and I had seen about birds of paradise; think we saw it after coming home from the Easter Eve service last year. Wonderful images, great footage of the kind that had never been shot before, going into a remote area on an island where there are many birds of paradise, including one that does a wonderful shimmying dance to attract a mate. For the first time, they shot footage of the shimmying bird from above—a bird's-eye view of the sort a potential mate would see—and discovered that from that perspective, a stunning flash of color appears when the bird, which is otherwise black, does its dance. Something in there for pondering—the otherwise hidden beauty that appears when we find a different view.

The documentary also included the Marvelous Spatuletail—a name you so liked. Lovely to come across the show again as I was preparing to wing my way up here.

Speaking of the Marvelous Spatuletail—that was one of the curious book things that happened. A small synchronicity, not quite on the order of Raymond Carver showing up but something to note, nonetheless. On our honeymoon, I had picked up a lovely, small book called *Birds* in one of the bookstores we browsed. Over time I had slowly been savoring my way through it (lovely plates, much like the huge book you bought for me, only much smaller), and it's still on my bedside table. Hadn't touched it for months. When I opened it sometime after your death, I realized I had left off just before an entry about the Marvelous Spatuletail. A splendid bit of synchronicity. As if you were winking at me.

—SATURDAY, JULY 19, 2014—
Toronto

A strange night. Sally and I had planned to drive down to the boat today (where Craig has been the past couple of days), so I had it in mind to make sure I got to bed at a good hour last night. I did get to bed at a good hour, but I turned off my light later than planned and think my brain and heart were still whirring when I finally did. I lay awake for a while, then turned the light back on and opened *Moon Crossing Bridge* again to read the next poem or two.

One of them was the poem "Moon Crossing Bridge," which gives the book its title, and in reading the poem, it finally hit me—*For Pete's sake, another bridge.* Of course, I knew *bridge* was in the title, and I had read the poem at least a couple times before. But that was probably before I really began to take notice of bridges appearing on my path. Here's the poem:

Moon Crossing Bridge

If I stand a long time by the river
when the moon is high
don't mistake my attention
for the merely aesthetic, though
that saves in daylight.
Only what we once called worship
has feet light enough to carry
the living on that span of brightness.
And who's to say I didn't cross
just because I used the bridge in its witnessing,
to let the water stay the water
and the incongruities of the moon to chart
that joining I was certain of.

I turned out the light again and continued to lie awake for a long time. Brain and heart felt astir with all of a sudden really seeing the bridge image in Tess's book—a book that has been important to me these past months. And feeling very aware of you. At one point I had a sense of you laughing (your wonderful laugh), taking delight in these connections I am making. At another point I realized the moon—a nearly perfect half-moon—was right outside my window, haunting and beautiful with just a bit of a haze blurring it. It was shining so intensely, I wonder if it contributed to my wakefulness. I got up and opened the blind to look at it, then left the blind open and lay in bed in the moonlight for a while before closing the blind again. Finally fell asleep in the late wee hours and got just a few hours' sleep before my alarm went off at 6:20.

Disappointed and frustrated to get so little sleep, particularly leading into a day we'd planned to go to the boat (three hours' drive each way), but also aware that the night held some enchantments with its poetry and moonlit bridges and connections and your laughter, and it felt important to be present to those enchantments.

I got up after my slice of sleep, had breakfast, and had just gotten out of the shower when Sally said she had talked to Craig. He'd reported that the weather wasn't great at the boat and was likely to continue in that vein all day. We decided to change our plan and are hoping next weekend will bring better weather. I dressed and went downstairs and talked with her a bit more, trying to figure out what direction to reorient myself toward. Decided to go back to bed for a bit! Glad I did. I read for a little while and then set my alarm for maybe an hour. Kind of a strange way to begin the day, but I felt much better for it.

The real gift of that extra sleep this morning—the last thread of the night's enchantments, perhaps—was that I dreamed of you. I remember only a bit; don't know if it was part of a longer dream or if it was simply a brief dream with not much else to remember. Bittersweet when I woke and remembered the dream, but I was glad to have seen you. It came as a gift.

And now for sleep, hopefully longer tonight but not without enchantments. May we meet on the bridge.

—MONDAY, JULY 21, 2014—
Toronto

Crosby, Stills, and Nash playing on the sound system at the café this morning. Makes me think of your friend Steve, who worked with them, and the day we received the news of his untimely death. How you said something along the lines of how he had been here in the world, living and breathing and creating, and now was in a box in the ground. The note that rang in your voice—was it futility? I remember it as having a feel of, *And it all came down to that?* though am not sure that's quite what you intended. But I thought of that conversation sometime after you died, with something of the same sense. It all came down to this? And so soon?

I want to trust it means more than that; that your dying is not the absurd, abrupt final word; that it didn't all come down to that moment in the hospital room when we released you, didn't come down to this awful grieving that those of us who love you have to live with every day; that somehow you are still living and breathing and creating, still crafting your story and your stories, only now with material at hand that we can barely imagine from here.

Last Thursday, talking with Christianne. Something we were talking about prompted me to think about Caravaggio's painting *The Incredulity of Saint Thomas*. I talked about this painting with her, how it struck me that as Thomas peers into Jesus' wound, he seems to be thinking, *There's another world in there*. I talked with her about my sense that this is something of what I'm doing right now: attempting to peer into the wound, to feel my way into it and through it, to feel the awful rawness of it and also to discern where it might be leading me. This wound—the wound of your dying, the wound that I feel afresh every morning when I wake once again to a world that does not have you in it—doesn't feel like a place of being stuck, though it's sometimes nearly impossible to imagine how to go on without you.

This is what I scribbled on an index card after talking with Christianne: *Connection with how I am seeking to enter into my grief. Reaching into the wound—not to wallow or hide in it—but to discover the world it leads to.*

And you? What world are you finding? Is there a place we can meet in the passage? Are we already doing so? Perhaps that's part of what these words are. A place of meeting. A bridge.

Another conversation with Christianne, several weeks ago. Told her about hitting a wall when I was praying, not knowing how to pray for you, and how, upon praying that, I immediately thought of Clarissa Pinkola Estés's story about the wounded wall—the story you had jotted notes about on that small scrap of paper I had found just before that.

Christianne and I talked for a while about walls. She asked if I had an image of the wall I had come up against. As I pondered that, I began to think of a wooden wall, something like the one Clarissa evoked. My wall is made of old, weathered wood, like the kind of wood you imagined working with one day—wood that you would reclaim to make cool crosses in the style of Irish high crosses, and to make a dining table for our home, and other things you had dreamed about that I knew were going to be wonderful, once you had space in your life to do such things.

I told Christianne that the wall was layered. Graffiti, perhaps, on the first layer—some things I had to say, to vent, to scrawl, some choice words about being without you. But also layers of blessings. Something came up about holes in the wall. We had been talking about bridges, and Christianne said it felt like the holes in the wall were a kind of bridge in themselves. And talked about the receivings I've been experiencing—the weird things with books and such—as being like notes you've passed through the holes in the wall. Loved that imagery she offered. It's especially easy to imagine things like the scrap with Clarissa's words being a note you've passed through the wall. These things that feel like gifts from you.

I talked, too, about how the kind of wall I'm imagining could be dismantled to make a bridge. Also imagining sparrows on top of the wall, planting seeds in the holes. Thought of the Western Wall in Jerusalem, where people place their prayers in the cracks of the walls.

I pray these words come to you like notes, like prayers, like blessings I'm passing through the wall to you. That somehow they reach you, that they find their way to you, that they come to you as a gift in return. That the notes passed back and forth will make the wall more thin, more permeable, until the day it is a wall no more.

Not sure I was aware of it at the time, but I did finally notice the connection between the Caravaggio painting and the wall—the wound in Christ's side, the wounds in the wall. The holes, the gaps. How a wound can become a place of passage, of connection, of beginning to find our way into another world—a world that lies within our own world.

When I read Christian Wiman's *My Bright Abyss*, I was struck by how he writes, toward the end, about going to a retrospective exhibit of works by Lee Bontecou:

> In every single sculpture from Bontecou's early work there is a hole, a space of utter blackness. The holes aren't included within the sculptures so much as inflicted upon them. They are expressions—the word seems wrong, for they are pre-expressive—of meaninglessness, little abysses that contain every last bit of the nothing that is space.
>
> The holes are in the later mobiles too. You have to look a bit to see them because the entire pieces are in a sense full of holes, and the singular expressions are very much a part of that total transparency. But they are there in every one, just as in the earliest pieces: that inexplicable, irreducible, and necessary hole that no art, this art clearly says, can ever completely fill....
>
> ...Art can model the more difficult dynamic of transfiguring one's life, but at some point the dynamic reverses itself: *life* models, or forces, the existential crisis by which art—great art—is fully experienced. There is a fluidity between art and life, then, in the same way that there is, in the best lives, a fluidity between mind and matter, self and soul, life and death.... It has to do with standing in relation to life and death as those late Bontecou mobiles do, owning an emptiness that, because you have claimed it, has become a source of light, wearing your wound that, like a ramshackle house on some high, exposed hill, sings with the hard wind that is steadily destroying it.

That last image he builds to, of the wound like a house singing with the wind that is destroying it—stunning. And emptiness becoming a source of light. So much there to chew on as I think about the gaping holes that your death has opened in my life and as I think also about the places of mystery and unknowing that I have come up against in your own story.

Some weeks ago, I scribbled this on an index card:

The gaps where I am missing or forgetting or never knew pieces of your story. Writing my way around them, like the Celtic monks did with pages of vellum that had holes; they wrote their way around the holes. The gaps became part of the landscape of the page, of prayer.

Of course, using the pieces of vellum that had holes would have been driven, most likely, by the monks' frugality, by their desire to waste nothing. Even so, I'm drawn to the images of sacred texts that incorporate the holes—the wounds in the page.

—TUESDAY, JULY 22, 2014—
Toronto

So when I did some searching yesterday, I couldn't find any images of the Celtic manuscripts with holes that I was thinking of; am wondering if I'm misremembering that they were Celtic. Will check a few books when I get home.

Did come across some other wonderful things in my searching—other medieval manuscripts with holes and other damage, and intriguing and imagination-stirring images of books from across the centuries. Found wonderful images on a marvelous site hosted by Erik Kwakkel, who's a medieval book historian at Leiden University in the Netherlands. Two of the images depict pages with holes that have been charmingly mended with embroidery. He writes:

> Holes in the pages of medieval books are common. They were easily made (by the parchment maker's knife).... Fixing it by stitching the hole together with strings of parchment is also common: parchment makers did it all the time, leaving behind "scars" on the page. What *is* totally unusual, however, is the repairs seen in this 14th-century book in Uppsala,

Sweden. The damage is repaired, or at least masked, by good old broidery. It was done by the nuns who purchased the book in 1417. It is delightful to think that they took the effort to make a medieval hole disappear by replacing it with patterns like this, made up from pieces of silk in the most vivid of colors.

I am enchanted by the tender, artful attention given to the book's wounds. These are such wonderful images of what can happen when we approach our wounds and the wounds of the world with beauty and care and creativity. These images quicken my desire to be intentional about what I do with this grief and pain and loss, this rending, this unfathomable hole that has opened up in my life.

Went for a long walk in Sally and Craig's neighborhood this morning, and as I walked and prayed, I found myself thinking, *What's the invitation?* That question has been such an important, core question for me for a few years, though when things become complicated and overwhelming, it can take a while for me to remember that question, to allow it to come to the surface. Right now, the invitation feels primarily like more of the same: writing, resting, walking, spending time with friends and family, entering into quiet and prayer and listening, meeting with Christianne. Tending the wound. Finding the artful threads that will help transform it.

Feeling drawn—invited—also to give attention to the rhythm of my days as part of the tending I'm doing, which will involve stretching myself in a new direction. Had a good conversation with Christianne about that last week and came away from it with some clarity and intention—not to make any drastic changes but to work in particular on how I enter the day, which for now primarily means making sure I have some time to write in the morning. And also working on not being up till all hours, which makes it too easy to get a late start in the morning. Hard to reconcile my night owl ways with the desire to get up and moving in the morning. But hoping to shift into a rhythm that enables me to continue to be a night owl, within reason, and still be able to enter the day before the morning is nearly gone.

One more image for you for today. This is another one I found on Erik Kwakkel's site when I was looking for images of medieval books with holes yesterday. In this one, a dragon looks out from a hole in the page that precedes it.

In the accompanying post, titled "Brilliant Damage," he writes:

> Parchment often contains some kind of imperfection. Holes, for example, are a common occurrence on the page of a medieval book. The parchment maker's knife, scraping off hair and fleshy bits from the animal skin, was sometimes handled with too much pressure, producing holes such as the one seen in this brilliant image. That a drawing of a dragon should perfectly align with such a hole is a coincidence. What I like about it is the view it opens to the next leaf. I can just imagine how the heartbeat of the medieval reader sped up when he saw that a dragon was about to be introduced into the story. Parchment damage as a sneak preview: excitement coming to a chapter near you.

The image resonates with my questions that have begun to stir about wounds and holes as passages, as portals. This image prompts me to ask not only where the wounds will lead us but also what they will help us see. How will we peer through the brilliant damage to find what lies beyond? Admittedly, this might be strange and scary. But it just might turn out that the dragon is friendly, the gatekeeper to a world that waits for us.

At the end of the last writing session, it occurred to me that part of what I'm doing here in my writing and praying and listening is finding a language, a vocabulary for engaging my life; a vocabulary not only of words but also of images (a visual vocabulary), of metaphor and story and poetry and dreaming; a vocabulary that will help me navigate this strange and foreign terrain. And if you abide, if you really are stirring in this world and slipping notes through the wall, perhaps it can be a shared vocabulary, a shared language, a place of meeting and of conversation—not at all as I have understood conversation in the past and as it happens in the rest of my daily life, but a place where something is offered and exchanged between us. A space of communion.

Some time ago—several months?—I had a sense of you wanting me to know that my imagination can be a place of knowing you, that my imagination has always been a gift and that it can be a gift especially now. I don't know entirely what that means, but I have a sense that the vocabulary thing is part of it, that drawing on these images and poems, learning the language that they can teach me, is crucial to my path right now.

I think again of my resistance to reading grief literature, as good as it may be. From nearly the start of this wrenching journey I have had a sense that the best medicine for me, at least for now, is to be found elsewhere. Poetry was my first inkling of it, via Raymond Carver and then Tess. I am coming to see more clearly that this is where my path seems to be leading now and where the invitation is: not to shy away from my imagination but to engage it with intention and artfulness, to open it to the wisdom and solace and inspiration and guidance waiting to be found in poems and art and story—that of other folks as well as creating my own.

The words and phrases that have bubbled up to the surface the past months—I think these are part of the vocabulary that's been taking shape, without my quite knowing at the time: *Listen. Ask. Receive. You must be very still.*

I also had a sense, very early on, of God or you wanting me to know: *You have all the time in the world to go a little crazy.* I took this to mean that while it's important to stay grounded and to give my attention and energy to what will be helpful and healing (and figuring out what that is in the first place), I don't have to be so concerned about making sure I'm moving forward in my grief in the way I might have previously thought moving forward looked like. That keeping it together is not the most pressing thing.

The language I'm gathering includes a visual vocabulary of images that have been surfacing, like these:

Bird
Wing
Bridge
Nest
Wall
Seed
Wounds
Holes
Gaps

It includes books, poems, stories, and particular authors such as these:

Raymond Carver, starting with *All of Us*
Tess Gallagher, especially *Moon Crossing Bridge*
Christian Wiman, *My Bright Abyss* and some pieces
    from *Every Riven Thing*
Clarissa Pinkola Estés's story about the wounded wall

Perhaps what I'm building is not only a language, a vocabulary, but also a kind of library—something that has structure, a space for gathering up resources that kindle my imagination. A space that perhaps can be shared with you, in however subtle a way. A place of meeting, of communion. I think this notion of structure, of an infrastructure that we are creating, was the first thought that came in this vein today that led to thinking about language and vocabulary—this body of poetry and stories and words and images that has begun to come together, seemingly for some purpose.

And this too: a blessing as a place of meeting. How might blessings be part of the vocabulary, the language, the library?

—WEDNESDAY, JULY 23, 2014—
Toronto

Yesterday was the Feast of Mary Magdalene. On Facebook I shared "The Magdalene's Blessing," remembering so vividly how I was sitting next to you as I wrote that blessing while we flew across the country toward Seattle for the women's convocation. Remembering that the workshops I led, for which I composed the blessing, were titled "Illuminating the Edge: Threshold as Sacred Space." What a big, fat threshold I am navigating—we are navigating—now.

Today, as a follow-up, I posted a link to our video *The Hours of Mary Magdalene* so that folks could hear your song "Mary Magdalena." In the process of sharing the link, I watched the video again so I could listen to the song. *Achingly beautiful*, I described it on Facebook. Hit all over again by the loss: of your voice, your astounding creative gifts, your presence in this world.

The night I was gathering up some of your archives to take to Gainesville with me, I went through a few of your notebooks. Some of the earlier ones have song lyrics mixed in among calculations for jobs you were estimating. In a later notebook, I was delighted to find a page with these words:

> Room service at the Warwick Hotel
> The silver and white linen
> We can pour the wine
> And dine by candle glow
> It's cozy on the 23rd floor
> Way up above the city
> Maybe later we'll step out
> And take in a show
> But baby maybe we could just stay in

Loved coming across this. Figure it was a song you had spent a little time noodling on during or after our honeymoon. I was grateful to receive it. Like a note passed through the wall.

One of the first novels I read after you died was *The Perfume Collector*. I happened upon it during a browse at the library, in the New Books section. Imagine my surprise when I began reading the book and discovered that part of the story takes place at the Warwick Hotel. Think that might have been the first weird book thing I noticed.

—THURSDAY, JULY 24, 2014—
Toronto

Noontime, and I finally got myself to the café just a few minutes ago. Felt like a huge accomplishment. Have been dragging yesterday and today. Lots of gray weather yesterday, which I'm sure had an impact. Cleared off beautifully yesterday evening, which helped. Had an especially nice and relaxed evening with Sally and Craig; that helped also. I made Mommaw's sausage casserole; turned out very tasty. We had some time on the deck after supper. Took a short walk with Sally and Sammy. Enjoyed a FaceTime visit with Scott and Lacinda. Grateful for all that. Felt my gloom starting to descend again at bedtime, though not as pressing as it had been earlier in the day.

Yesterday was the first time I'd made Mommaw's sausage casserole since before you died. You really liked that casserole. Everything so laden with memory, so many firsts to navigate, again and again and again. Making things you liked. Going to a movie for the first time since you died. Small things to large.

But it's sometimes the small things that feel most fraught, can trigger sorrow so easily. I always miss you, but it's typically in the everyday stuff that I miss you the most—and enjoyed the most with you. Waking to you, moving through the day with you, sharing meals with you, being back and forth in each other's studios, running errands with you, climbing into bed with you at the end of the day and then waking to you again the next morning.

I don't want to romanticize it; there was difficult stuff too, but even in the difficult, whatever shape it took—to know we were together, that you were on my side and I was on yours, walking through every day together and trusting it would somehow all work out. How is it supposed to work out now?

How can you catch the sparrow? Crosby, Stills, and Nash are singing over the sound system.

Some thoughts from my session with Christianne yesterday:

I sent her the writing I did on Monday and Tuesday of this week, when pieces were coming together about vocabulary, language, a library being built. A good conversation about that. She asked what felt significant about this, and I talked about how it seems like a space where I can gather up these discrete experiences I've been having—the weird stuff with books, the ways you seem to be showing up, as well as the words, books, poems, images that have become important—and bring them together so that they don't feel simply like separate experiences but have some relationship to one another, *become* something when they're seen together. It feels like they have some purpose; they have some kind of space to them that becomes a means of engaging my grief and also, perhaps, a place of meeting you.

Christianne said that although I have lots of questions about what the individual experiences actually mean—are they you? are they coincidences?—all these things are going into a structure that I'm saying is important. A helpful insight. I don't know what the individual experiences mean. But they do seem to be serving some purpose, and this language, or library, that is emerging seems authentic and helpful and, in some way, real.

I talked also about how the language feels like a kind of unlocking, that it provides insight and knowing. And in saying that word *unlocking*, I was reminded of the conversation I had with Karen, Kathy, and Barbara just a couple weeks or so after you died. I talked about how I had been, so unwillingly and so suddenly, handed this "process" that I was stuck with, that although I had some choices about how to enter the grief, there was no getting around the fact that I would have to be in it now. And I felt like I was locked into it and resented that enormously. Hugely. Completely. I told them how I'd been thinking about keys—that in the midst of feeling locked in, I wanted to find some good keys that would help me feel less locked in, less confined and bound.

Later realized that we were in the midst of the Advent days of the O Antiphons, and the antiphon on the day we had that conversation, or maybe the day after, was this:

O Key of David and Scepter of the house of Israel, who opens and no one shuts, who shuts and no one opens: Come, and bring forth from prison the captive who sits in darkness and in the shadow of death.

Curious timing.

It was helpful yesterday to think back to that conversation, to make that connection, and to feel like with beginning to perceive the coming together of a language or vocabulary or library, I had found a key.

Christianne and I talked also about light. She said something about sensing the presence of light in this language, this library. I thought of illuminated manuscripts, that perhaps this is a library of illuminated manuscripts. Pages and words that shine in the darkness. Told Christianne about the medieval manuscript that's sometimes called the Black Book of Hours. It was created on black parchment, which causes the gold to shimmer and the colors to be so vivid. I first saw an image from it in Roger Wieck's book *Painted Prayers*; feel sure I showed it to you at some point. Came across it again a few nights ago while doing that search for images of medieval manuscripts with holes in them.

Christianne asked me if I had an image of the library; what does it look like? I go back and forth between thinking in terms of language and vocabulary—less structured—and the more structured image of a library. Both seem to be a place or means of meeting, of communicating, of being in communion. I have some shadowy images, not clear at all, but I have a sense of the library as being like a chapel. A warm and inviting space. I shift between thinking of it as open and airy and light-filled, and as darker, more like one of those centuries-old English libraries, with lots of corners to explore or curl up in. I imagine the library with secret passages. Tunnels and places of connection. Told Christianne also that I imagined it kind of like the Weasleys' tent in the Harry Potter series—much larger and more wonderful on the inside than it appears on the outside.

Somehow that was linked with talking with Christianne about driving to South Florida to see Peg and Chuck over Epiphany. It was just a month after you died. On the drive down, I had an intensely physical sense that I was being hollowed out—I could feel it in my chest, that it was actively happening. As I paid attention to it, the words came to me—not audibly, but so very clearly: *This is the space you will need to hold him now.* It helped enormously. It didn't fix anything about your being dead. Didn't make me feel any better about the awful wrongness and horrible pain of it. But it helped to know that the sensation of hollowing had some purpose to it. That there was still something I could do. That I could hold you, whatever that meant, and means.

I remember thinking, sometime after that, about that tent in the Harry Potter book and had a sense that in the small space of my chest I was holding a whole world—worlds, even. And that it would be a place where I could endlessly explore. Like a library with nooks and treasures and secret passages and all manner of things to be discovered, only even bigger than that.

You're holding worlds this year, Christianne said to me as we talked about these things yesterday. Yes. I think she said this shortly after I talked about how coming to recognize this language, vocabulary, and library thing felt like part of the point of taking this year to do what I'm doing (not that I will be finished in a year's time). That without entirely understanding why, it felt important to cancel the in-person events you and I had scheduled this year and to give myself what Peg and Chuck called (during that Epiphany visit) *extravagant permission* to do what I need to do in this initial year of grieving. Even though it's sometimes difficult to allow myself to do what I feel like I need to do in this time, I still feel fiercely protective of this year and giving myself the space I need to be present to the grief in a creative and mindful way.

The language and library realizations that came this week felt like a confirmation of the importance of this. I don't think I could have come to those realizations if I hadn't given myself the space I need right now, including taking this time away from home, when I'm able to be present to the grief in a somewhat different way, a way that seems possible only when I'm not at home, where I am constantly confronted with the force of your absence. I am always mindful of your absence, always carry the sorrow of that, but it is different here, in this space that doesn't have memories of you so attached to it.

Told Christianne also that I could imagine you laughing in delight at the library thing, rejoicing that I had finally gotten it, finally seen it. Told her that if you abide, it must surely be in a place where these kinds of recognitions and connections come so easily, a place where you can see so clearly and this kind of stuff is constantly happening, that it's part of your language, part of your way of being now. But it takes me longer to come to these connections, particularly when the grief can so overlay everything and hinder me from seeing what's before me. I trust the grief also sharpens my sight, that I see differently than I did before.

But that doesn't make it worth it. The seeing is not anywhere close to being an adequate trade-off for not having you here. I talked about that too with Christianne yesterday, that even as I can take some delight in coming to an awareness like I have this week with the library, nothing about it changes the fact of your being gone.

I always come back to that: You are gone. You are dead, and I will never see you again in this life, never know you as I have known you. I can be open and pray and look for connections; I can work to find the keys that will help ease, ever so slightly, the abiding sensation of being locked into this grieving process; I can bring my art and writing to this path to help me engage it and transform it; I can entertain ideas about what might yet be possible. But I do not want to be on this path in the first place, do not want to have to reckon with the unremitting awfulness of your being gone.

—FRIDAY, JULY 25, 2014—
Toronto

I talked recently with Christianne about how living with (living through) the grief involves allowing some layers to grow over the horror I feel over your dying. I used the word *veneer*, though, as I told her, that's not quite the word. It wouldn't be healthy or bearable to constantly live in the rawest place of my grief. But sometimes, something pulls back the veneer, or it just falls away on its own, and I am revisited by the raw, horrifying awareness that you are dead.

I think of the last moments with you, of having to let you go. I see the awful red incision that traced along your scalp. I think of the paralytic they administered during your final night as they made last-ditch attempts to save you, and I still feel the sense of suffocation I felt when they did that, as I wondered whether you had awareness of it—whether being medically paralyzed felt different than being in the induced coma or the sedation that came later.

I learn to cope. I learn how to keep breathing. I let some layers of veneer or bandages or whatever settle onto the most raw places of memory. But underneath it all, horror and rage and feeling lost and an awareness of being so *without* you, that you are so unbelievably gone.

I hold God responsible in some measure, and I don't trust God so much right now, and it makes no sense that you are not in this world—that Emile has lost you and I have lost you, that your father and Dee and your brothers have lost you. The graces and blessings that come do not absolve anything; they do not relieve God of responsibility. They make some things more bearable, but they do not erase the horror or justify your death.

I am grateful for the hints that come—that you might be stirring, that you might be offering some connection—and I want to stay open to these. At the same time, they serve to underscore how gone you are, how paltry it seems to strain to discern an echo of your voice as compared with being able to hear it, in the flesh, every single day, talking and singing and laughing and calling my name.

This Monday I fly back to Orlando. Three days, and I will be back in our home. There is a measure of comfort in this, but also a sense of dread at being back in the place where your absence is present with such force. Will be leaving for Minnesota two weeks after that and think that's a good thing. To be able to touch base with our space, our home, but also to know that I'll be able to have some more time away from it before long.

PART THREE
Show Me Your Face

MAP

I will make a map
to you.

I will make a map
to you.

It will be
of feathers,
it will be
of stones,
it will be
of twigs
and the very
lightest
bones.

I stopped by the downtown library yesterday. My first time there since before you died. First time going alone in I don't know how long. I went in search of a couple of poets who surfaced while I was in Toronto.

On my way to the poetry collection on the fourth floor, I was lured into the Friends of the Library bookstore. As I browsed the shelves, my eye was drawn to a book titled *My Mistress's Sparrow Is Dead*, a collection of love stories. And whom should I find in there but Raymond Carver, with his story "What We Talk About When We Talk About Love."

I emailed Christianne last night, told her about finding the book. *A sparrow and Ray*, I wrote, *one fell swoop*. I don't know if it was you stirring, but I was glad to see Ray (and the sparrow) turn up again, especially at the end of a hard week. I had, in fact, planned to order the books I was looking for but felt spurred yesterday to go to the library instead. Glad I followed the impulse.

—Monday, August 18, 2014—
St. Joseph, Minnesota

What if *I* abide?

Christianne invited me to consider this at our most recent session, a couple of weeks ago. *Abide* is a word I often use when I talk about you with Christianne. *If he abides*, I say to her, meaning *if he lives, if he continues, if I will see him again*.

Talking about this, she asked, *What if you abide?*

She spoke of lingering, of rest, of manna—these things I am seeking to do or be or ask for in these days. The question went straight to my heart, flew like a bird into that space in my chest that I hold for you. It gave words to what I am trying to do: to listen, to ask, to rest, to move in a way that enables me to see what I need to see. And there's that second meaning as well: how *abide* can mean not only *to live, to dwell*, but also *to bear, to endure*.

Thinking about how I might abide in these days, I talked with Christianne about how the word speaks to taking care of myself in healthy ways, finding rhythms that will bring healing, and also how it seems that moving in this way—finding these healing rhythms—will also draw me into rhythms and cycles of time where you and I might connect. Holding that not as the primary goal but wondering if in our abiding, as we each learn to move and live in new ways, we might find places of connection and crossing—that we might abide this awful loss by learning how to abide together, across the distances.

—Tuesday, August 19, 2014—
St. Joseph

I sometimes wonder if you are trying to connect all the time, speaking clearly, but I receive it in such a partial fashion, either because I am still learning the language or because of whatever natural barriers of time and space are in place. What I get may be jumbled or seem unclear, but I hope that whatever is there, whatever you might be saying or wanting me to know, I am somehow absorbing through my skin or my heart or by whatever means possible.

Thinking about this writing I'm doing here, this talking to you and to myself that I am doing in these pages, I am coming to think of this not only as a meeting place—part of the library that I began thinking about in Toronto—but also as something that is taking on a kind of substance. Not firm, not structural, precisely; I think of it as something like the passage from Revelation where John offers this beautiful image: *When he had taken the scroll, the four living creatures and the twenty-four elders fell before the Lamb, each holding a harp and golden bowls full of incense, which are the prayers of the saints* (5:8).

You and I were both drawn to that image and to the notion that somehow prayers can take on substance, even if that substance is as ethereal as incense. This writing, these words, these pages feel like they are made of something of the same stuff, that in their intent and their repetition, they are taking on substance, becoming something that somehow connects us, however subtly. A kind of skin, perhaps. Or a veil. Or perhaps the reality is somehow reverse, that each word, each page, works to wear away the veil, the wall between us.

Hm. Taking on substance, or wearing it away?

Whatever the case, I pray that somehow you know these words, or at least the heart from which they come. That you feel the force of the loving that gives rise to every word.

—Thursday, August 21, 2014—
St. Joseph

Struggling with the sorrow, which has been especially keen the past couple of days. Had a quiet and sad morning at Mary's, trying to figure out what would help. One step was to do a Facebook post. I shared a photo of a sparrow who crossed my path in Toronto, and also these words:

> Gary and I were especially fond of Psalm 84, where the psalmist writes, "Even the sparrow finds a home, and the swallow a nest for herself, where she may lay her young, at your altars, O Lord of hosts." Brenda read it at our wedding, and again at Gary's memorial service. The psalm was also a favorite of the ancient Celtic monks, who often spent their lives in perpetual peregrinatio (pilgrimage). I can imagine the beautiful imagery of the psalm captured their longing for home, and their desire to find it in God. I'm struggling these days to know where home is, and so this psalm is speaking to me anew. It seems like sparrows have been attending me ever since Gary's death; they were all over the place in Toronto, and now here in Minnesota. They come as a comfort. Here's one of them for you. May it bring you comfort and good cheer and a glimpse of home.

I've received some lovely responses. Glad I posted. The responses have helped me feel a bit less lonely today.

This afternoon I walked to the library at Saint Ben's. Went in search of Kevin Young's *Book of Hours*. Spent some time with it. A couple of poems that struck me:

GRIEF

In the night I brush
my teeth with a razor

And another one with the same title:

GRIEF

The borrowed handkerchief
    where she wept

returned to me months later,
    starched, pressed.

Drawn to the brevity of these; so much grief evoked in so few words. In the first poem, I'm struck by the severity of the image; in the second, the restraint. How they each speak so much of grief.

In my last session with Christianne, I talked with her about coming across an anthology of poems about grief and loss while browsing a bookstore and how I didn't feel inspired to purchase it, how it felt like too much to have so many of these poems in one book, that it was more helpful for them to come to me one by one. She said, *Yes. These poems have been coming like manna—and the whole book of grief poems feels like a feast that you would gorge on, when manna is what's needed.*

In a dream two nights ago, we were floating on a river that, in the dream, ran down the county line road where I grew up. You were on your back, and I was resting on top of you, belly to belly. I remember hardly anything about the dream except that we were moving along the river on the part of the road just after you turn onto it from 441. You were keeping me afloat as we drifted along.

When I dream of you, I usually don't hear your voice; not sure what that's about. I think we talked a bit in this dream. I don't remember what you said, but I remember it being reassuring. That I was going to be okay, that you had me.

Oh, Sweetheart. I am weeping as I write this. At the time of the dream, it didn't seem monumental, other than that I woke up being so glad I had seen you, as I always am when I dream of you. But I think of the river and how you were holding me up, speaking to me in your calm and reassuring way, and I miss you so much. I trust that somehow you are holding me up and we are moving together—perhaps that's something of what the dream was about, giving me an image of that. But I want you *here*.

It didn't occur to me till now, writing this, to think of this in connection with the river in *Big Fish*. I had seen Emile perform in a musical production of it the night before the dream. (Sweetheart, your boy was amazing.) There is a powerful, beautiful, heartrending scene right near the end, where Edward, the father, is dying in his hospital bed.

The river, he says to his son. *Tell me how it happens.*

How what happens? his son asks.

How I go.

The son—who had not, until then, understood his father's stories and their power—says he doesn't know that part of the story but then begins to tell it, with his father's help. The telling takes them down to the river, where all the characters from the father's stories are waiting to welcome him. So incredibly powerful. I had tears streaming down my face then, as I do now.

Sweetheart, were you welcomed like that? Were there beloved

faces waiting to meet you? Friends, family, maybe even some of the folks in your stories—Uncle Tabernacle and his sister, Glossolalia; or Bon and Tell, from the story you were in the midst of writing when you died; or any of the folks from the beautiful stories you would weave through your Song Chapel concerts: Jacob and Jonah, John the Evangelist, Mary Magdalene? Or friends like Steve or Joe or Gamble? At the last, when your breath gave out and your heart, unbelievably, stopped its beating, were you gathered in at the river or some other place of gladness?

I hope, Sweetheart. How I hope.

And I pray that you will help bear me up, that you will bear me along, that you will stay in the flow with me.

—Friday, August 29, 2014—
Tybee Island, Georgia

I have been thinking tonight about what a good eye you had, how often you spotted things that I might otherwise have missed: a deer by the side of the road, a cool bird, the new moon. You had an eye for the moon; I loved that about you. One time we were driving somewhere, on one of our retreat trips, somewhere up north; we had just turned onto an entrance ramp to the interstate, and you said, *Did you see that?* I said, *See what?* You said, *It was some kind of little brown animal, just standing by the on-ramp.* I said, *Was it waving at you?* You thought that was funny and would sometimes tell that story. I think we learned it was a gopher.

I loved how you saw me. From the very beginning.

What might it mean to see you now? To open my eyes fully to who you are—to see as much as I can about the entirety of who you have been and who you are now?

These words from Henri Nouwen on "The Companionship of the Dead" came my way today:

As we grow older we have more and more people to remember, people who have died before us. It is very important to remember those who have loved us and those we have loved. Remembering them means letting their spirits inspire us in our daily lives. They can become part of our spiritual communities and gently help us as we make decisions on our journeys. Parents, spouses, children, and friends can become true spiritual companions after they have died. Sometimes they can become even more intimate to us after death than when they were with us in life.

Remembering the dead is choosing their ongoing companionship.

There is a sliver of moon in the sky tonight, waxing. I pray that you, with your eye for the moon, still see it. I pray that you, who gave me the most extraordinary gift of seeing me, still see me. I pray that I might see you and know you still.

—TUESDAY, SEPTEMBER 2, 2014—
Gainesville

You are nine months gone today. A very bizarre gestation period. It always feels like a moment and an aching eternity since you died. There is so much I want to share here with you from conversations with Maru, Christianne, and Peg and Chuck, and also from conversations that unfolded on Tybee this past weekend. Would love to have lingered there with the gang for a few more days. But it's good to be in Gainesville. Mom and Dad and I are meeting your dad and Dee for lunch at Scott's shop at Tioga tomorrow. Haven't seen them since Family Christmas and am looking forward to the visit.

For today, I wanted to offer at least a small gathering of words. To tell you I love you. That I pray you will teach me, show me, something about the kind of time you are living in now.

This got me thinking about your song "The Art of Time" from *KATZ*, the one-man show you wrote and performed at the Orlando Fringe Festival years ago. I have your archive here in my bedroom at Mom and Dad's, stacked in plastic boxes on the other bed. I just spent the past hour or so going through some of those boxes in hopes of finding the lyrics. I found them:

The Art of Time

The most important day
Of anybody's life
Becomes a memory of a memory
That fades away
Why have you brought me here
I only have to leave this life
Always forgetting, and letting go
Of another day

The stars are in the heavens
For a billion years
And even their light will one day fail
All the stars in the heavens
Fragile as our tears
Are diamonds of the evening sky
And I will dry these tears from my eyes
'Cause I will always believe in my heart
That you will teach me
The art of time

Now and forever
Beginning and the end
Eternally

The most important ones
That ever walked this world
Are temporary, contemporary
And then on their way
What do you want from me
When you know that I must love this life
How will I shed it, and not regret it
And just walk away

Good grief. *You know that I must love this life / How will I shed it, and not regret it / And just walk away.*

I always loved this song. Not sure there's a recording of it; need to go through your box of videos and see if *KATZ* was taped.

Also came across a file of old photos of you! Wonderful to see them. Mostly head shots, including some shot in 1991.

A treat to come across those photos on this night, and grateful to find your lyrics for "The Art of Time." Please teach me, Sweetheart. Teach me something about the time you are living in that will help me bear the time I am living in here.

— THURSDAY, SEPTEMBER 4, 2014 —
Gainesville

In our Skype session today, Christianne commented on how she and I have often talked about how you might be reaching through the membrane into my world, stirring these synchronicities that have been happening. She went on to say it had occurred to her to wonder how I am passing through the membrane, entering into *your* time. I was so struck by this. Do you experience me entering into your world? Is that part of what's happening here, in this writing? Do the notes being slipped through the holes in the wall between us go both ways?

We talked a lot about time today. I told her about looking for the lyrics to "The Art of Time" last night and shared your words with her. I told her about how I experience this writing space as a place where, in the midst of what I imagine are our very different experiences of time, you and I somehow meet; our time-arcs brush against each other, cross, open.

I talked also, or tried to—it's difficult to articulate—about my sense that you are entering deeper and deeper into my marrow. Or perhaps were always there and I'm becoming more intensely aware of it. But it does feel like a deepening. That I get to hold the whole of your life—including, somehow, the nearly five decades that you lived before I knew you. (Did I ever not know you?) And that holding the whole of your life includes holding your life now, whatever that means, whatever that is, whatever I might know of it. In my marrow, where you are making your home.

—SATURDAY, SEPTEMBER 6, 2014—
Gainesville

I went for a walk this morning. It was raining so very lightly. As I walked, I thought of that night soon after your first surgery, after everything went so terribly, horribly wrong. I had come home to try to sleep. In that space before sleep, words floated into my consciousness; my memory is that I could actually see them in my mind's eye: *slow rain, slow rain.*

I wrote about that in one of my reflections for the Advent retreat. This is part of what I wrote: *After a few minutes it occurs to me to wonder if this is something of what Gary is experiencing. A place of slow rain; a space where time has altered, has slowed, has become unbound by chronology.*

And so I let the slow rain fall on me today, praying you were somehow in it.

I pray to know something of that altering of time in this life. I pray that time will expand for what I most need to do and to be. I pray that you and I will find openings in time, places where we can have some knowing of one another.

—SATURDAY, SEPTEMBER 13, 2014—

I drove back to Orlando on Thursday and brought back a few things from your archives that I had left in Gainesville this summer, including the eight audiocassettes you recorded as you were working on some of your songs.

On the drive, the first song I listened to was one I didn't readily remember, which was unusual. It tells a story from the perspective of a woman who, with age, is losing her memory. It drove me to tears; terribly poignant and sad, especially on this side of your death. *They've taken him beyond me / And I have carried on*, you sing.

I listened to the cassette a little bit longer. Everything else I heard was familiar; snippets of songs in progress. Intriguing to hear them at an earlier stage of their development, and a fascinating glimpse into your creative process. Also a heartbreaking one, thinking of all the songs you still had in you. I hope you're getting to write them now.

I made it home in time to quickly unload the car before heading over to Christianne's. An intense but good session with her, as they always are. What a godsend she is. Literally.

I told her about listening to your tape, about beginning (while I was in Gainesville) to scan some of the photos from your photo collection that covers so much of the span of your life. She referred back to our conversation last week and asked how I am experiencing the *nowness* of you. Working with pieces of your past seems somehow part of how I am experiencing the *now* of you. I talked about how, if you abide, then who you have been is still, presumably, part of who you are now and that working with the tangible pieces of your past—like your photos, especially from the time before I knew you—perhaps gives me glimpses into not only who you were but also who you are now.

I was reminded that one of my prayers these days is *Show me your face*. I'm not even sure exactly what that prayer means, but it has something to do with knowing you still—as you are now, whoever you are now. Though it's painful, there is also something wonderful about seeing photos of you, especially the older ones—seeing something of the face that was yours then.

After I came home from Christianne's, I spent the next few hours searching for something—a tape, a CD, a video—that might have "The Art of Time" on it. I went through some boxes in the garage, I went back through much of your studio, and though I found other treasures, including several old tapes of you singing, I can't find anything with "The Art of Time." I'm starting to despair I'll ever hear it again in this life but am holding on to some hope it might yet turn up, perhaps on one of the videos or CDs of your performances—most of those are still up at Mom and Dad's.

But here's the best part. In my obsessive searching Thursday evening, I went through a bin in your studio. I had glanced in it before but evidently hadn't gone through it very far. It seemed to be something of a catchall bin. As I dug further, I came across a whole collection of your handwritten song lyrics; not sure how far back they went.

Mostly they were familiar ones from more recent years, but there were some things I wasn't familiar with. Including, notably, the lyrics to that first song on the tape that I had just listened to for the first time earlier that day. These are the lyrics I read:

Waving hair a garden
Whitest flowers that grow
In the spring she won't forget
Of so long ago
Of so long ago

How in this world can I help you?
This world so far away
From the one within your eyes
Oh yesterday
Oh yesterday

Will I finally save him
My one and only love
They've taken him beyond me
And I have carried on

In her wheelchair
This winter afternoon
The sun upon her
Fading all too soon

When she sees me
She sees someone else
Someone who was there with her
Someone who could help

We were never lovers
I was too young
Let me finally save him

Those last three lines were at the top of the page; my recollection is that you sang the refrain again at the end. The melody is beautiful and haunting, a Celtic feel to it.

How remarkable to discover the lyrics on the same day that I heard the song for the first time. Another mysterious synchronicity.

Found a couple other beautiful treasures in that box—handwritten song lyrics, unfinished, that you were working on. This:

How can there be flowers
How will they ever bloom
The winter is upon us
And covers everything
When the days are weary
Under winter skies
I keep a watch for flowers
Believing in the spring

A little bit of ribbon
A little bit of lace
The day you wear your wedding dress
The look upon your face
Oh the look upon your face

Put your hand upon my breast
Feel the beating of my heart
You will find the truth of me
I will walk beside you
Wherever this life leads

One day I'll pop the question
I swear that day will come
I will not turn upon this road
Until that day is won
Until your hand is won

And so will I be blessed
To stand beside you on the day
You wear your wedding dress
You will wear

And then it breaks off. But how extraordinary to find this.

And oh, my love, those words: *Put your hand upon my breast /
Feel the beating of my heart / You will find the truth of me / I will walk
beside you / Wherever this life leads.* I thought, of course, of the day
you died, when I placed my hand on your chest—my hand upon
your breast—and commented to the nurse, *It's so strange to feel a
heartbeat and know it's only my own pulse*, and she said to me, *His
heart beats in you now.* I thought, too, of all those times, lying in
bed, when I would put my head on your chest and listen to the
beating of your heart, your incredibly strong heart.

Sometimes at night, when I'm praying, I'll place my hand over
my own heart, and listening to it—listening to your heart beating
in me—is itself a prayer.

Sweetheart, I want to know the truth of you, still; to feel the
beating of your heart, still; to know you walking beside me, still.
Wherever this life leads.

This treasure appeared in the box as well—a torn scrap of lined
paper with these words in your handwriting:

Orange blossom honey
Sweetest honey in the world
Oh my orange blossom honey
Orange blossom honey girl

That was all, but how marvelous to find that! What a spectacular fragment.

The next day, yesterday, I had a visit with Sue. At the reception after your service, she had handed me a small jar of orange blossom honey. On the label she had written the words, *The sweetness remains!* She mentioned this as we were leaving Infusion yesterday and said she didn't know why but had felt inspired to bring it for me that day. She also said that Scott (I think I had given the jar into his keeping at the reception) told her it was my favorite honey. In that moment yesterday, I couldn't tell her about having found the "Orange Blossom Honey Girl" fragment just the day before, though I'll tell her sometime soon. Another marvelous and mysterious synchronicity.

And another synchronicity: On the scrap of paper with the orange blossom honey lyrics, you had written, at the top, *Ghost orchids—Fakahatchee Strand.* I did an online search and discovered some things about ghost orchids at Fakahatchee Strand Preserve State Park in South Florida. I wonder what prompted you to make that note; perhaps a seed of an idea for a song or story? Something about the ghost orchids captured my imagination.

Then this evening I spent a few minutes on the front porch. I had taken a book of poems out there with me, *Come On All You Ghosts* by Matthew Zapruder. I wasn't familiar with him; it was one of the books I came across in the poetry section at the downtown library a while back. In the second poem, titled "Aglow," I found these lines:

No one can know what they've missed,
least of all my father who was building a beautiful boat
from a catalogue and might still be. Sometimes I feel him
pushing a little bit on my lower back with a palm
made of ghost orchids and literal wind.

Ghost orchids, twice in forty-eight hours.

Are you in these synchronicities? Any of them, or all of them? It's hard to fathom you would intentionally take it upon yourself to send, for instance, ghost orchids my way. Is all of this—from the first time Raymond Carver showed up, in January, down to this week's ghost orchids—simply a beautiful coincidence? A particularly intense and extended stretch of synchronicity of the sort that perhaps happens all the time but that I am especially sensitive to right now, in my state of grief and longing?

Or perhaps sending me ghost orchids—and sparrows, and Raymond Carver, and Tess, and so forth—is exactly the kind of thing you're up to right now, finding inventive and unexpected ways to tug at my attention and imagination.

If you are in fact in these synchronicities, what's the point? What's the invitation? Are you simply seeking to offer comfort and reassurance? Or are they happening for some other reason, some other purpose?

One last synchronicity, a small one. While I was waiting for Sue to arrive at Infusion, I browsed through their shop. With the refrain from your song "I Have Carried On" still echoing my heart, I came upon a porcelain pendant bearing these words: *Carry on.*

I'm working on it, Sweetheart. Though sometimes the kind of carrying on I want to do is the other kind: weeping and wailing and making a scene. Curious—I just looked up *carry on* at the Merriam-Webster site to see how they define the term's shades of meaning. This is one of the two examples they give: *She bravely* carried on *despite the loss of her husband.*

Please help me carry on, Sweetheart, in whatever sense I need.

—Sunday, September 14, 2014—

For weeks I've wanted to write about my visit with Peg and Chuck at the Minneapolis airport. We had such a marvelous conversation, and I wish I could reconstruct it all, but some of what I took away was a real lifting of my spirits and a sense of vision and energy about the first book of blessings I'm starting to work on, especially in conjunction with the consultation I had with Christianne about the book some weeks prior.

I made a few notes during our conversation about the book of blessings. Chuck had some beautiful things to say about how you are a part of the creative process with the book. I feel this clearly. You are deeply intertwined with the book; you and I talked so much about it, and you were so much a part of every blessing. This is a source of comfort, but it also makes working on the book challenging. But gaining clarity about the book has helped to stir some energy and make me feel less overwhelmed.

Chuck talked about the book being a place of spaciousness—a place for the reader to lay their grief down and rest a while.

I wish I could remember more precisely the next part of my conversation with them; it just about set Peg and me to weeping. Chuck said, *Imagination equals love. You are stirred, and your words stir others to reimagine their own stories.*

And somehow you were in all that. As we finished that part of the conversation, I asked Peg and Chuck if they would lay their hands on the binder that has nearly all my blessings in it and offer a blessing of their own. We each put our hands on the book-in-the-making—the book that, I sense, already exists in some way—and I was so aware of your hands as well, both absent and present with ours. By way of blessing, Peg said *Gary*, and Chuck said *love*. And a few other things, but those were the main things.

On another note, a couple of nights ago I pulled John O'Donohue's book *Beauty: The Invisible Embrace* from the stack on my nightstand. I had picked up the book at Tattered Cover when we were in Denver several years ago (I think you bought it for me) and had started reading it, I think, soon after. I hadn't opened it since sometime before you went into the hospital.

I felt drawn to return to it and flipped through the index to see if O'Donohue had written anything about death in there. He had, in the penultimate chapter, "The White Shadow: Beauty and Death." Some intriguing things in there, including this:

When someone you love is dying, your sorrow is for the loss of them and the loss of the world they carry. Eternal life must mean that neither the person nor their world is lost. Eternal life must mean the continuity beyond death of that individual life and that individual world.

Eternal life must also mean that one day we will be together again with the ones we love. This is the beauty of the notion of resurrection. In much contemporary thinking there is the tendency to view death as a simple dissolution whereby the body returns to mother earth and the spirit slips into the air to become one with the universe. While this claims a certain elemental continuity, it cannot be described as the eternal life of the individual. This view would accept death as a reversal and unravelling of the mysterious and intricate weaving of an individual life and it seems to offer very little. Indeed, all it delivers is a bland description of death as an elemental physical process. The intimacy and mystery of the individual life is merely loosed into anonymous, vague energy. In contrast, the resurrection promise is the continuity of the individual life in transfigured form. We will be ourselves. We will recognize each other and we will be together, reunited for eternity.

I pray he's right. I was just telling Christianne, in our session last week, that I'm not enamored of the notion that the afterlife involves being absorbed into some cosmic, ethereal state. That holds no appeal. I'm really taken by the idea of incarnation: that we are given particular bodies, that this is how we know the world and embody the divine. From this vantage point, I don't want to be absorbed into some disembodied universal oneness—though I grant that if that's how it goes, it's likely different, and hopefully better, than I imagine it. But I hope it doesn't go that way.

I hope Paul is right when he writes in 1 Corinthians 15 that in the life to come, we will have bodies and that they will be transformed. That we will be embodied in some fashion: less burdened by them, less weighed down and prone to suffering because of them, and more easily able to live into their marvels. I think of something Lesley's mother said when she was so sick, before her death; she talked about the verse where it says we are fearfully and wonderfully made. *I understand about the fearfully made part*, she said. *Now I want to understand the wonderfully.*

Most of all, I want to know you: to know you in your wonderful particularity, to know that who you are has not been lost but is dwelling in eternity with utter freedom and grace and love, unhindered by the things that weighed you down. I want to recognize you and to touch you again. I want to look into your eyes and hear you call me Sweetheart and Beloved. I want to hear you sing again.

There is still resistance in me and some measure of disbelief that there is anything after this, that you abide beyond this life, that I will know you again. But in the face of all these synchronicities and with the deepening sense of knowing in my bones, in my marrow, it seems increasingly difficult to hold on to the disbelief and to hold out against the mysteries and possibilities.

I think again of the blessing I wrote just days before you went into the hospital, the "God of the Living" blessing, and marvel all over again at how every line, every word speaks into my experience now. Holding on to this especially this night:

Then may you be given
a glimpse
of how weak the wall

and how strong what stirs
on the other side,

breathing with you
and blessing you
still,

forever bound to you
but freeing you
into this living,

into this world
so much wider
than you ever knew.

—Sunday, September 21, 2014—

Gorgeous light in this early evening. You should be sitting here on the porch with me, at the end of a weekend spent together. We should be talking and dreaming about what lies ahead, in the way we sometimes did on this porch. There was something about sitting alongside each other and looking outward that inspired those kinds of conversations: about where we might live, what kind of home we might have, how our vocation would unfold. I loved those conversations, loved dreaming and imagining with you. Loved beginning to live into those dreams with you.

We had a conversation, not so very long before you went into the hospital, in which you asked, *Would you be interested in reimagining our life?* You didn't know quite what you meant by that, but even as you asked it, I could feel the question dancing around inside me. It was such a difficult slog for you—all you had to deal with in booking the concerts, all the time it took away from writing and creating. My heart leapt at the thought of reimagining with you, prayed that there would be a path that would lead you from having so much of your energy consumed and drained away by the parts of your vocation that weren't life-giving.

So I'm sitting on the porch where we used to talk and dream— the porch that provides just barely enough shelter from the hard rain that's begun—and I think back to your question, *Would you be interested in reimagining our life?* and it chills me. This is not the reimagining I had in mind for us.

And you, what are you imagining now? Do you imagine? Do you dream? What is your life like? Is there discernment and envisioning and reimagining involved for you now? Is there anything we can still dream or imagine together?

In our session on Thursday, I shared with Christianne that I've felt some kind of internal shift this week. This happens frequently; I always seem to be entering a new room in the House of Grief. But this felt a bit different, more pronounced. I told her it felt like some recess of my soul had just gotten the news you had died, that the fact of your death, your being so gone, was settling into some deeper layers. This week brought a more acute sense of *This is my life now*. I know—or I'm trying to trust, at least—that the grief won't always be so desperately sharp. But for the rest of my earthly life, I am going to have to wake up every day to a world that doesn't have you in it and figure out how to get through every moment without you here.

—SATURDAY, SEPTEMBER 27, 2014—
Asheville, North Carolina

Thursday was a chaotic day; leaving for a trip is always challenging, and this one was especially so. I have set out on a long-planned road trip that will eventually lead me to Toronto. I don't know just how long I'll be gone, only that it's time to go.

I spent Thursday night at Mom and Dad's. Before I left the next morning, I went into your archives I had stashed there and grabbed a handful of CDs in hopes I might find "The Art of Time" among them. I popped in the first CD as I left Gainesville. It was a compilation of songs from various live performances. When I heard the third song—"The Trial of the Hypnotist," a very cool song from *KATZ*—I was hopeful, and sure enough, the next song was "The Art of Time." I wept as I listened, both in gratitude to be hearing a song I had begun to despair of hearing again in this life and also in heartbreak that you are not still here, writing your amazing songs.

I spent much of the drive listening to you. You created an extraordinary body of work, Sweetheart. It was heartrending but wondrous to listen to you. It was the most I'd let myself listen to your songs since you died. But there seemed something important about hearing your voice as I drove the road to Asheville, remembering so clearly making the trip here with you last November. I found myself wishing that somehow, in tracing the road we traveled, I could undo the events of last November and December, could reverse the awful course that led to your dying.

There were some other treasures among the CDs—several other songs I wasn't sure had been recorded, including "The Trial of the Hypnotist," "The Righteous Live by Faith," and "Albert Einstein and the Book of Hours," also from *KATZ*. I was especially glad to hear that last one; I had wondered whether there was a recording of it.

So I've launched out, Sweetheart. I'm officially on my Big Road Trip. How I wish you were with me. Though I wouldn't be on this trip if you were still here—but you know what I mean. I wish you were here in this world with me, in the flesh, traveling through this life with me. Please show up in whatever way you can as guide and traveling companion on this road. I pray this trip will be an occasion of gaining both clarity and a deepening sense of the mystery in which you—and I—live. I pray you will meet me in both the mystery and the clarity, bearing their gifts in each hand.

—Tuesday, September 30, 2014—
Asheville

Met Daniel Nevins for lunch today at a Jamaican place called Nine Mile. Hadn't seen him in I don't know how long. Years. Good to catch up with him. Lots of talk about paradox and mystery and such. At one point he said to me, *Your work was never there to lessen the mystery.*

Early in the conversation, just moments after I sat down, he said something about how difficult Ordinary Time must be. Yes. Exactly. It's what I've told several people: No matter how hard the high seasons are, I have some sense of what to do in those seasons—how to plan, where to be in order to get through them. It's the

Ordinary Time that kills me, that I find the most difficult and painful. Waking every single morning to a world where you are not and having to figure out how to make my way through a day in which I will not see you, touch you, hear you. Not in the flesh, at least. Hopefully in other ways. But not in the ways I have counted on.

We talked about the dead. Daniel said something like, *We never go anywhere; we're always here, just in another form.* I talked about reading John O'Donohue recently, his lovely words about how the dead help us and how grieving involves attuning our hearts to sense their loving nearness.

I wonder if you are truly near, if you are on this journey with me, and whether you even know that I am traveling, that I am on the road, that I am trying to find my way and learn what it means to live in this life without you here. How much do you know about me now, about my life? What are you able to see and perceive? But even in the midst of my questions I find myself remembering a moment from this morning, doing something ordinary like brushing my teeth. I was thinking about these synchronicities that have happened this year and how some of them felt like they were for the purpose of assuring me that you remember me, that you remember our life together, that you have not forgotten.

Daniel mentioned this poem by John O'Donohue and sent it later today:

FLUENT

I would love to live
Like a river flows,
Carried by the surprise
Of its own unfolding.

Pasting it here just now, I thought of the dream I had some weeks ago of us floating down a river, belly to belly. In this awful unfolding, Sweetheart, may we become fluent. May we be wise to the river that is unfolding for each of us. May we be wise to one another. May we find a language in which we can be fluent with one another, even as we find the flow of this new life that we never expected, never wanted to face at this point in our journey.

—WEDNESDAY, OCTOBER 1, 2014—
Asheville

This afternoon, Brenda and I walked around downtown Asheville. We browsed through Blue Spiral Gallery. It gave me pause, thinking of how you and I had done that four years ago.

Came across one piece—I don't recall by whom, but what struck me was the title: *Keeping*. The word tugged at my imagination. These past months have been so much about the anguish of letting go. Seeing the title today, I found myself wondering, *What do I get to keep?* It doesn't fix anything, doesn't make me feel better, but it might be a good question to hold at this point. *What am I keeping?* And perhaps these as well: *What are you keeping for me? What are you keeping with me? How are you keeping me?*

A couple weeks ago I watched small pieces of the video of your show *These Dreams That Fly*. I was floored by the last song; I think it's titled "Only the Journey." I watched you sing the song and then watched how, at the end of the song, you put away your guitar, stepped into the circle formed by all the actors who were in the show, and spoke these words from the song:

> If we had only seen the road
> That lay before us
> We would have surely turned away
> But deep into the dark, dark night
> We drove and we drove
> Until we found the light of day
>
> It's only the journey
> The open road
> It's only the journey
> That brings the traveler home

Then you drank from the bowl that the actors had passed around the circle as you sang, and then you said, *Bring me home.*

And I wept and wept, for so many reasons: for the song's terrible beauty and poignance; for the road that lay ahead of us that we couldn't have known; for having to travel through this dark, dark night without you; for how homeless I feel; for the hope that you found a sense of home in the life we made together; for the hope that you are now fully at home. I wept for things I can barely articulate but that so pierce and lay open my heart.

Watching you on the screen, I suddenly realized I could see my reflection alongside your face. You were singing the song a decade before I knew you. But somehow I had always known you.

Praying to know you still. To know you always. To know you again.

Praying that you will be with me as I travel farther down the road tomorrow and every day to come.

Praying that you will help me find a home in this world.

Praying, Sparrow, that you will help me find a nest. That you will shelter me still.

—TUESDAY, OCTOBER 7, 2014—
Toronto

I am angry. The anger has often been present, in varying degrees, since early on, and it is coming to the surface again. I find myself awash again in the futility of your death, what a waste it seems, how absurd it is that you are not here—with me, with your son—and creating your amazing songs. I've paid attention to the anger, have talked about the anger, have prayed with the anger, but even that seems futile. The anger seems intimately intertwined with the absurdity of your death, with the ridiculousness of your being gone. Mostly the anger is directed toward God. While I don't believe God caused your death, I can't help but hold God responsible for not saving you, for not protecting you better during the surgery, for your not being *here*, in this life with me, doing what it seemed we were born to do and to create and to offer together.

It doesn't feel like paying attention to the anger makes any difference. The anger won't change anything about your being dead. I want to trust that paying attention to the anger will change something about me in some helpful direction. But right now, paying attention to how angry I am just makes me more angry, and sad. I am weeping as I write this and think part of it might be the journey catching up with me—the journey of the past ten months as well as the preparations and travels of the past couple of weeks. I have been looking forward to this road trip and know it's where I need to be right now, but what comes after it? I know some of what comes. But the daily stuff, the living of this life without having you here— there are times the weight of it seems nearly unbearable.

I miss you. It always comes down to that. I can savor the synchronicities and imagine this library and language we're creating, I can be grateful for how you seem to be stirring on this side of the veil, but nothing compares to having you here, to walking through this world with you.

Maru sent this poem from Rumi in a recent email:

> The breeze at dawn has secrets to tell you.
> > Don't go back to sleep.
> You must ask for what you really want.
> > Don't go back to sleep.
> People are going back and forth across the doorsill
> > where the two worlds touch.
> The door is round and open.
> > Don't go back to sleep.

I had this poem on my mind sometime in the past couple months, so it was lovely to receive it from her.

You must ask for what you really want. What do I really want? *All I want is you* comes to mind from the beautiful song you wrote for me a lifetime ago. Just a few weeks after we began dating, I left for New Mexico for nine days, for some events that Alexander Shaia had invited me to lead. You dropped me off at the airport and began writing a song on the way home. You recorded it to a cassette and sent it to me via FedEx:

> Sunny days and the nights are clear
> People come and they go
> As anyone can easily see
> I've got a million things to do
> But all I want is you

But if I can't have you, in the flesh, in this life, then what do I want?

—THURSDAY, OCTOBER 16, 2014—
Toronto

A number of things have converged in the last week and a half, more so than usual (if that's possible). Last week, Monday to Thursday, was the Residents in Ministry retreat, which you and I should have been leading. Last Thursday should have been a Wellspring evening. Last weekend was Canadian Thanksgiving weekend, which stirred memories of the last Thanksgiving meal I ate: on Thanksgiving evening last year, Scott, Lacinda, and nephew Scott brought leftovers from the Evinston feast, and we had Thanksgiving dinner in a corner of the hospital cafeteria.

As this year has unfolded, I've been aware when an event was taking place that you and I had planned to lead. For the most part I haven't given a tremendous amount of thought to those events, in large measure because I felt so confirmed that not going was the right thing to do. But this one—the RIM retreat—felt different; I think it had much to do with the fact that it was the final event, other than the Advent retreat, we had scheduled for this year.

I had a session with Christianne last night and talked about how the RIM retreat last week prompted the sensation that I've been moving through a ghost year this year—that there was a year you and I should have had, and didn't get to, and in some ways the RIM retreat marked the end of the ghost year. It became the last event we would ever schedule together in this world.

I spent some time on Sunday and Monday working on a new blog reflection for the week. Having already written a reflection on the lectionary's gospel text some years ago, I decided on the Exodus text, where Moses asks to see God's glory and God hides Moses in the cleft of the rock. As I worked on the artwork and reflection, I found myself gripped by the story. I started thinking about that word *cleft* and how it comes from *cleave*, which, paradoxically, can speak both of rending and of union. That's the direction I went, and I wrote a blessing called "In the Cleaving."

Also while I worked, I found the words *cleft of the rock* tugging at my memory, thinking there was something about this in the Song of Songs. Sure enough, I found this, in Song 2:14:

> O my dove, in the clefts of the rock,
>   in the covert of the cliff,
> let me see your face,
>   let me hear your voice;
> for your voice is sweet,
>   and your face is lovely.

Let me see your face, let me hear your voice. It is almost exactly what I say to you each night, and sometimes at other times as well: *Show me your face, let me hear your voice.* And sometimes it's exactly the wording of the Song: *Let me see your face, let me hear your voice.*

The passage falls immediately after one of the texts we selected from the Song for our wedding:

My beloved speaks and says to me:
"Arise, my love, my fair one,
   and come away;
for now the winter is past,
   the rain is over and gone.
The flowers appear on the earth;
   the time of singing has come,
and the voice of the turtle-dove
   is heard in our land.
The fig tree puts forth its figs,
   and the vines are in blossom;
   they give forth fragrance.
Arise, my love, my fair one,
   and come away."

Immediately preceding the verse about the cleft of the rock, the bride says this:

My beloved is like a gazelle
   or a young stag.
Look, there he stands
   behind our wall,
gazing in at the windows,
   looking through the lattice.

It's hard to describe the sensation I had when I read this chapter from the Song, noticing the *Let me see your face, let me hear your voice* piece and its proximity to one of the passages from our wedding. Noticing also the presence of the wall, window, and lattice, given the imagery of the wall that emerged in recent months—the wall where you seem to be passing notes through the holes. And the connection with the cleft of the rock, as I continue to feel so keenly both senses of the word *cleave*.

As I noticed all of that, it felt like something shifted in me. Those threads in the Song—the threads between the Song and the Moses story, the threads between the Song and our life together—

felt akin to the synchronicities that have been taking place throughout this year, but they also felt somehow different.

One thing I noticed and talked about with Christianne last night was that with many of the previous synchronicities, there was some element that appeared from outside my experience, something I wasn't already familiar with or that wasn't part of my daily life, like being drawn to the Raymond Carver book of poems or finding myself outside a shoe store listening to a friend talk about sparrows. With the Song, it seemed like the synchronicity took place deep within the landscape of my life, using elements that were already part of my life. It made connections between what was already there, in the sacred text of the Bible and in the sacred text of my story and ours. It felt like we had found a secret room in this library we seem to be creating.

There was something more to the shift, though, as if perhaps a few more strands of doubt fell away. And in their place, a deepening sense that you are indeed at work in my life and that this is how we talk now, using these texts and images and poetry. I haven't laid aside all the questions and doubts, but certainly there is something at work. Whether it is specifically you or whether it is some other kind of synchronicity, clearly something is stirring that is beyond my experience and comprehension.

Help me to keep my eyes open, Sweetheart. And help me find some solid ground in this torrent of emotion—in the sorrow and weeping, in the anger and weariness.

In my sleeping, in my waking: *Let me see your face, let me hear your voice.* And in this cleaving, please help me experience the union more than the rending, the connection more than the tearing apart.

PART FOUR
We Are the Thin Place

BIRD

A bird in the hand,
worth two in the bush.

And a bird on the wing:
what would you give?

A heart,
a heart,
a heart.

Well, Sweetheart, it's Halloween. I am in a cozy bed on a cold night (snow predicted tomorrow!) with Daisy the cat curled up beside me. It is quite a fine place to be. But I should be with you, curled up together, having celebrated the occasion of our first date.

I drove here yesterday from Pennsylvania after spending several pleasant days with Janet and Adrian at their lovely home near Gettysburg. Grateful for that space of quiet companionship.

Early in the day I drove through part of Catoctin Mountain Park, which was beautiful. At some point—perhaps after I had passed through the park—I put on one of your CDs I had listened to on the day I drove to Asheville weeks ago, as I began this Big Road Trip. It was the CD that's a recording of a concert you did in 2002. I made it okay through "The Trial of the Hypnotist" and "The Art of Time," but then when "Gamble Rogers, You Have Spoken" came on, it undid me, and I had to turn off the CD. Many tears ensued, and some yelling at God. I'd never had that kind of reaction to that song before. I think at least part of what was going on was that it got me thinking about both you and Gamble dying so prematurely and what a waste it seems that you are both gone from this world, where you should be living and breathing and singing songs and telling stories.

It was a hard day, a hard drive. I felt kind of guilty about that, because so much of it was so beautiful, and it seemed small of me to feel sad and angry when I was driving through such beauty. Sometimes, in this year of grieving, I have thought of this Chippewa song that I first came across many years ago:

> Sometimes
> I go about pitying myself
> While I am carried by
> The wind
> Across the sky.

In those times when I feel guilty for feeling sad or sorry for myself amid the beauty of the world, I think perhaps the most I can hope for is to be able to notice the wind carrying me across the sky and to be present to the life and beauty amidst what has shattered. I don't think feeling guilty about feeling sad or angry or sorry for myself will stop me from feeling sad or angry or sorry for myself. I think the way through all that will come in paying attention to the difficult and painful emotions while also trying to remain present to the grace and gifts that come my way.

In a recent conversation with Christianne, I talked about how mindful I am that even though my grief feels huge, I'm so aware of those whose grief is intertwined with terror and all manner of hideous suffering. My grief seems small in comparison to this. And Christianne said, *But this is what's breaking your heart now.* Yes. This horrible being without you that breaks my heart all over again every single day.

So it was a drive laced with tears and rage yesterday. But then I finally arrived in Asheville last night, and Brenda and Catherine immediately set about to feed me and make me laugh. They did more of the same this evening after they got home from work. So grateful for them.

Sweetheart, it is midnight. All Hallows' Eve is turning into All Hallows' Day. The Feast of All Saints. Here on this threshold, I ache for you. I rage. I weep. And I carry such joy for the extraordinary gift of loving and being loved by you, for the sheer wonder of it, for the marvel that our paths ever met and joined. I hold it all this night and always: the aching and raging and weeping, the joy and the wonder, the love that flows beneath and through it all. May that love both bind us and free us.

In these days, Sweetheart, may the veil be especially thin. Please slip some more notes through the wall. Or just punch some holes in the wall, that it will feel less like a wall and more like a place of meeting.

—Saturday, November 1, 2014—
Asheville

We woke to snow this morning! Lovely to have snow on All Saints.

It is nearly midnight, turning from All Saints to All Souls as I write.

I had a Skype session with Christianne yesterday afternoon; we had originally been scheduled to meet on Thursday, and I'm glad that, due to my travels that day, we wound up rescheduling for yesterday. Good to connect with her on Halloween, though the conversation was draining, as is often the case. But such a gift and a help to be working with her. She lights a candle when we meet, and as we closed yesterday's conversation, she said that as often as possible—without burning down the enchanted cottage—she would keep the candle lit for me throughout these three days. Lovely.

Yesterday I talked with her about how, for so many years, this trio of days has been a time when I'm mindful of how the veil thins toward the past. It's been a time of remembering, of thinking about other lives I might have had if I had made other choices, of letting some (mostly friendly) ghosts come to visit as I think about people who have been part of my life. (I'm so glad I didn't make any choices that would have caused me to miss you.) Just a few years ago, as I moved through Halloween/All Saints/All Souls, it occurred to me that the veil thins not only toward the past but toward the future as well. I don't recall specifically what I was thinking about in connection with that—what piece of my future I was pondering, though it might have been the year we got married, or perhaps the year after that, when I was looking toward the future with great delight. I began to think of this trio of days not only as a time of remembering but also of dreaming and imagining.

I shared this with Christianne, how that was a good awakening and shifting for me and how I want these days to be a time when I experience the veil thinning toward the future—to do some dreaming and imagining, to have a glimpse of how my life is unfolding or what steps I need to take next. But now, when I think about the future, mostly I sense darkness. I know that none of us knows just how our life is going to unfold, but the unknowing feels particularly keen and painful for me.

I talked with Christianne about how I have a sense of some of the pieces of my future that involve my vocation—things I'm glad to be working on and have energy for, such as the book of blessings, the online retreats, my blog. But when it comes to other stuff—the part of my life beyond work (though work is so intertwined with everything in my life)—it's difficult for me to imagine what might lie ahead. What will the rhythm of my life be like? How will I cultivate community? Where and how will I find a sense of home? There is so much darkness that attends these questions, so much that I can't see or even really imagine. I hardly know how to begin to imagine how my life will unfold. Feels like I am going to be traveling through a long, vast liminal space.

I pray that you will help me hold these questions. That you will hang on to me and travel with me as I wait for answers and go in search of them. That you will help me know how to pray, where to look for help, where to push and stretch, where to rest. That you will help me find home and create it. That you will somehow still be home for me and with me.

Near the end of my stay with Sally and Craig in Toronto, it occurred to me to wonder what it might be like to meet you in a place that's not so defined by grief, a place where sorrow is not my dominant emotion and my primary way of moving through the world. I think that place is a long way off, but I had a sense that just with noticing the question, that place had already begun to emerge. To my eye, it appeared as a tiny circle: a circle marked by light, by spaciousness, even though it's so very small right now. Something, at least, that has the capacity to become spacious.

It was intriguing to notice that question coming to the surface. What will our relationship be like as my grief becomes less excruciating and intense? People keep telling me it will happen, but it's hard for me to imagine. (And I remember sitting with Brenda in my studio back in March and how she told me, so helpfully, that it's not that I will stop grieving but that I'll learn how to weave your memory into my life in a new way.) How will we know one another then? Will you still strew some synchronicities through my days? Please do. Always. Even though I'm not certain to what extent you're taking an active hand in those synchronicities, they come as such a comfort and a source of wonder.

It was shortly after the question surfaced that I drove from Sally and Craig's to Janet and Adrian's. The drive took me through some really lovely areas of New York and Pennsylvania. The Susquehanna River kept me company for a good stretch; I fell in love with it.

At one point, as I was driving along a valley, I saw a tiny circle of sunlight on the trees that were thick on the side of the mountain. It was such a small circle; it seemed anomalous. I couldn't locate where it was coming from—presumably a small gap in the clouds that I couldn't see. As I drove on, the spot of light grew larger and larger before finally passing out of my range of vision. Particularly appearing so soon after I had begun to carry that question, which itself felt like a tiny circle of light, this sight came as a lovely gift.

It made me think of your song "Only the Journey," which has been much on my heart during this trip:

If we had only seen the road
That lay before us
We would have surely turned away
But deep into the dark, dark night
We drove and we drove
Until we found the light of day

It's only the journey
The open road
It's only the journey
That brings the traveler home

It's nearly 1:30 in the morning. All Souls' Day is well under way. And today marks eleven months since you died. Oh, my love.

Please inhabit these hours, this All Souls, this third day in this trinity of days, that it will become a thin place for me in a new way.

And please help me discern how the veil might thin toward the future. Inhabit my dreaming, my imagining, my discerning. Help me open my eyes to possibilities, doorways, new thresholds. Be a companion and shelter and guide on my way. Please do some dreaming with me.

—Sunday, November 2, 2014—
Asheville

Feast of All Souls. One hour till midnight. Grateful to have spent this trio of days in Asheville with Brenda and Catherine.

It was lovely to hear from people who remembered you in their All Saints' services today—who spoke your name or remembered you in other ways. You were included in the liturgy at Winter Park and Trinity and elsewhere this morning. Aaron and Dan had been in touch about using my poem "It Is Hard Being Wedded to the Dead" for this morning. I talked to Mom and Dad tonight, and I gather that your picture was included in the time of remembrance and that Dan shared something about you, I think in connection with sharing the poem. You were remembered.

I hate the fact that we had occasion to name you among the dead on this All Saints' weekend. In the midst of this, I am thankful for those who remembered you and who let me know this. I particularly loved the beautiful message from Ann in Atlanta, who described the banners that encircled her congregation that morning in tribute to the Great Cloud of Witnesses. She sent a photo of a banner on which she had written your name. She wrote, *How grateful I am that Gary's contributions in this life continue to give me a glimpse of the next.*

Mixed feelings, not surprisingly, about going home—though using the word *home* gives me pause, as the home we created together doesn't feel like home in the same way. I know it will be a challenge to return. But I received this email from Janice last week, after asking if she'd look in on the house:

Hey, sweetie—

It was a pleasure to walk through your home today and see how you and Gary *made* it such a beautiful space.... There is a sense of peace in that place that may be hard for you to feel right now, but know that it exists. I don't think Gary's gone yet. He loved you so deeply and so well, how could his spirit not remain for you a guardian?

I'm so glad you're spending this time away, but I do believe that you still have a sanctuary over there. I'm wishing you the peace that passes all understanding and the healing that seems still so far away.

It was such a gift to receive these words from her, to hear her name our house a sanctuary and a place of peace and that she senses you still there. Her words will make a difference in how I return to that place. Our home. I am praying that I will know you still in that place and that it will become home for me in a new way.

When I leave here tomorrow, it will be almost exactly a year since you and I drove home from here after Brenda and Catherine's celebration, just days before your surgery. At least I'll be veering toward Gainesville, so it won't be entirely the same route, but for the most part it will be the same road you and I took that day. Our last trip. I'm not looking forward to the drive but would really like for it not to be a miserable day. Please help me, Sweetheart. Let there be some sweetness in the day, some graces on the road tomorrow.

—Friday, November 7, 2014—
Gainesville

Last night, in my quiet time, I asked you to open up some thin places between us. Had a sense of you wanting me to know, *Baby, we are the thin place.* Sweet.

—Tuesday, November 11, 2014—
Gainesville

I'm leaving for Orlando tomorrow. Had thought about heading out yesterday, but with yesterday being exactly one year since you and I arrived home from our final trip together, I decided maybe that wasn't the best day to be traveling to Orlando.

On Thursday it will be seven weeks since I set out on this Big Road Trip. There's part of me that's feeling a tug toward home, in whatever way our house can be home for me right now. Another part of me feels some trepidation about returning, wondering what it's going to be like to return, especially as I move into this stretch of time that holds significant markers, including the anniversary of your disastrous surgery on November 14 and your birthday on November 17. Please move with me through these days. Please inhabit these days with me and breathe with me and carry me. May we be a thin place in these days.

—Thursday, November 13, 2014—

Am back home now, and it occurs to me that for all I've been thinking about the anniversary of your surgery being tomorrow, it didn't fully hit me until tonight that it means today, a year ago, was my last full day with you, my last day with you as I knew you, my last day of being seen and known by you.

That day a year ago, I wound up spending a chunk of the day

at my desk, working to organize the Advent retreat registrations that had come in. I spent more time than I had planned working on that, probably a combination of feeling the need to have that info together so that after you were out of the hospital and we were able to return to work on the retreat (so we imagined), it would be ready, and also, beneath that, most likely feeling a need to have some control over *something*.

You were at work too; not sure just what. And we did spend time together, but not as much time as I had intended to spend with you on that day. I apologized for this at the end of the day. You said, *We were together.*

I have thought of this so many times since then: the tremendous grace of your words, the truth of them continuing to cut through my lingering regret. *We were together.* No matter what we were doing, all throughout the time I knew you, we were together.

I want to trust that's true still: that you are still with me, still knowing me; that we are together still and always.

Sweetheart, it's been such a hard day in such a hard year. Hard to get out of bed today. Hard to keep moving. Hard to stay present. I miss you so much.

I had a session with Christianne this afternoon. Hard there too; wrenching but also good to have the hard stories held. Some ways into the conversation she asked if there was anything in connection with the day of the surgery I wanted to share. I didn't feel drawn to do so at first, but as I thought about it and began to respond, I wound up talking about it a good bit. That was hard but felt right. Sometime I'll write some of it here, but not tonight.

Another piece of our conversation prompted me to comment to Christianne that my grief over what I've lost is so acute that it can sometimes make it difficult to be open to what might still be possible, in terms of knowing you and listening for you. I know I'm in a different place with this than I was in the early days and weeks after your death, when you felt so abruptly and completely gone and I had no sense of any way you might still be with me as anything other than a memory. I felt such despair over the possibility I might never see or know you again. I still have many questions and places of unknowing, but I have less despair (though not less sorrow) and more hope.

I can't imagine ever being okay with your being gone. In the midst of this, I pray to be open to how I might know you in whatever way is possible, even as my life unfolds in new directions. How might I continue to know you in a way that's not clinging to our past but is part of leaning into our present and future (if we can even speak of time for you)?

I had a beautiful email from Scott yesterday morning letting me know he was sending thoughts and prayers as I move through the coming days. He offered to come down tomorrow, and I'm taking him up on it.

In the astounding sorrow, Sweetheart, I am so grateful that we were together. That somehow we are together, still.

—Friday, November 14, 2014—

Sweetheart, it is just after midnight (the morning of the 15th now). This time last year, we had been at the hospital for over twelve hours. Scott and Lacinda were with me, along with your dad, Dee, Jeff, and Suzanne. We had hours yet to wait before the neurosurgeon would come out and say, *It did not go as we anticipated.* Hours to wait before I would learn that my world, our world, had come apart.

I do not want to tell that story tonight. But I will tell you that today, a year later, was a day more lovely than I would have hoped.

Scott arrived a bit before noon. After I finally finished getting myself together—was moving slowly today—we headed downtown. Had lunch at Panera at Lake Eola, where you and I had gone any number of times for lunch or a cuppa—and of course a bear claw for you, most times, and a cookie for me. We began planning our first Advent retreat there. Today was the first time I'd gone there since you died. It was cloudy and gray this morning, cloudy and gray in the early afternoon when Scott and I left the house. But as we sat by a window at Panera, Scott spotted blue sky, and when we left, it was sunny and a beautiful day.

We drove to the Orange County Regional History Center, where Mom's cousin Pete Ballard has six of his fashion dolls on display as part of an exhibit about the movie *Gone with the Wind*. Then to our neighborhood Starbucks, which, in all this time, I had never been to. Pizza from Ragazzi's for dinner. Scott hit the road a bit after eight o'clock. So grateful for Wonder Brother, who made today better than I would have otherwise expected.

I had visions of climbing into bed early tonight but sat in the front room for a good while and fiddled around on this laptop, taking care of some emails and receiving the lovely comments that folks sent via Facebook, where I had written this post earlier today:

> Remembering Gary's surgery this day last year, I am especially praying for all those who will be involved in any way with surgery today.
>
> I am praying for the patients, that they will be encompassed with protection.
>
> I am praying for the surgeons, nurses, and anesthesiologists; the technicians, admissions staff, chaplains, pastors; and everyone else whose life will touch the life of someone in need of healing.
>
> I am praying for those who are waiting today: for family and friends who are moving through these hours with hope and concern. May the news that comes at the end of the waiting be joyous. And when it is not, may there be welcoming arms to enfold, console, uplift, and bless.
>
> I am praying.

And I am praying for you, Sweetheart. Tonight and always.

—Monday, November 17, 2014—

Your birthday. Are you aware of birthdays where you are? It turned out to be a really full day, which was probably good.

Was having a tough morning, so I called Barbie to see if she was available for lunch on short notice. She had sent a lovely email last week saying, *I am praying for you for the upcoming anniversary dates of Gary's surgery and his birthday and just your homecoming in general. Are you craving company or solitude? If it's the former, I'd love to get together with you whenever is good for you. I will also understand if you need time alone or with family right now.* Greatly appreciated her spacious invitation.

I was glad lunch worked out for her today; we met at Infusion and had a great visit. She even brought gifts, bless her fuzzy heart: a couple of things she had spotted and picked up for me. A beautiful scarf with birds on it (we agreed they're sparrows) and also a puzzle with charming paintings of birds—combining the sparrow/bird thing and your fondness for puzzles. Barbie is always so thoughtful, and I was really touched by her kindness and remembering the thing with sparrows.

Home for a little bit, having had a late lunch with her, and then met Emile for an early supper at Little Saigon. So grateful to see him on your birthday. I hadn't been to Little Saigon since before you died; I know it had been a long time for him as well. He came by the house afterward, and I gave him one of your guitars; a bittersweet moment, but it went well.

So, whew, that's the day. Your birthday. Draining but also lovely in ways I hadn't anticipated.

—Tuesday, December 2, 2014—
Gainesville

One year today. How have I managed to keep breathing for an entire year?

It is actually Wednesday morning, nearly 3:30 a.m. I have been staying up ridiculously late for days, tending the Advent retreat and the administrative onslaught that always attends the beginning of a retreat. There's something wonderful about the onslaught. But I am weary, weary, weary. Hope the pace will shift after the initial push of launching this week.

So am taking myself to bed, finally, but could not let this day end without writing something, anything, here in this space.

This is a poem that was posted in the online forum for the retreat today: a treasure from Ailsa Flynne, whom I have so enjoyed in previous retreats and who posts such lovely things on the forum:

"His heart beats in you now"
each pulse
a stick laid carefully in the sand
guiding you
through this shifting of worlds
towards a new constellation in your togetherness.

She wrote this in response to today's reflection, in which I drew on Daoud Hari's words about navigating the desert by sticks and stars. So I share Ailsa's lovely treasure with you as I finally head toward bed and rest.

PART FIVE
Book of Hours

Sparrow Sings the Hours

Matins
There are more doors in the dark
than you can imagine.

Lauds
I never get enough
of these stars.

Prime
Watch how we hold this day
in the palm of our hands.

Terce
If you could see
how you look in this light.

Sext
Still, still, we have
all the time in the world.

None
Listen while I tell you
everything I have not forgotten.

Vespers
Nothing now to do
but let yourself be gathered.

Compline
Hush now. Rest now.
I can carry this song all night.

For the past week I have been carrying the sensation that I have come to the end of a long arc that began with your death and continued through the Advent 2013 retreat, the Lent 2014 retreat, the travels of last year, and then the most recent retreats. Not the end of the journey by any means—there is plenty I am still carrying from the earlier arc—but definitely have landed in a place where much of the earlier work has been completed and I have some room to breathe, which is a gift.

The real marking of the end of this arc came last Sunday, when we gathered on the farm to bury your ashes. It still seems unbelievable as I write it. We buried your ashes. Emile, your dad and Dee, your brothers and their wives, Mom and Dad, and Scott and Lacinda—everyone I had invited. We gathered at the packinghouse at four o'clock last Sunday afternoon and, after a bit, made our way down to the lake, to the spot that I picked out on the Point, nestled among a small stand of palmettos. By design, it was a simple, brief ceremony; I had told our family beforehand that after going through your memorial service and the service at Annual Conference, it would be helpful to me that this not feel like another memorial service.

Scott—bless him—had prepared the site beforehand, and he and I drove down to it so that I could see it before arriving there with the rest of the family. He continues to be amazing and thought of everything needed for that day, including bringing in some better dirt to fill the hole, covering the dirt with camo cloth and palmetto fronds, and having a small platform for your box so that it wouldn't be on the ground—the beautiful wooden box that he built for your ashes.

When the gathering assembled down at the Point, I talked about how, when you and I were preparing for our wedding on the farm (just five years earlier; our anniversary was two days before we buried your ashes), the word *blessing* kept visiting me, so we were intentional about making it a day of blessing—asking particular people to offer blessings, and inviting those who have been such embodied blessings to us. I talked about how, as I had prepared for this day of burying your ashes, the word *blessing* had come to mind once again and that I wanted it to be a time of gathering together and offering blessings.

I shared this blessing with them. When I went to look it up, I was struck that I wrote it in 2013, for the last Ascension Day you would spend alive:

STAY

> *So stay here in the city*
> *until you have been clothed*
> *with power from on high.*
> LUKE 24:49

I know how your mind
rushes ahead,
trying to fathom
what could follow this.
What will you do,
where will you go,
how will you live?

You will want
to outrun the grief.
You will want
to keep turning toward
the horizon,
watching for what was lost
to come back,
to return to you
and never leave again.

For now,
hear me when I say
all you need to do
is to still yourself,

is to turn toward one another,
is to stay.

Wait
and see what comes
to fill
the gaping hole
in your chest.
Wait with your hands open
to receive what could never come
except to what is empty
and hollow.

You cannot know it now,
cannot even imagine
what lies ahead,
but I tell you
the day is coming
when breath will
fill your lungs
as it never has before,
and with your own ears
you will hear words
coming to you new
and startling.
You will dream dreams
and you will see the world
ablaze with blessing.

Wait for it.
Still yourself.
Stay.

Like a number of other blessings, this one reads quite differently to me now, on this side of your dying.

I told them of how I had a palm-sized stone engraved with your
name on one side and *Beloved* on the other side and had placed it

in the box that holds your ashes. I had similar stones engraved as keepsakes for Emile and me and gave his to him then. After that, I passed around smaller stones engraved simply with the word *beloved* and invited each person to take one.

I told them we used to close each Wellspring service with a blessing, and I led them in the kind of blessing we did with our Wellspring community. We held our left hands palm down, and I offered some words about this being a prayer that we would release whatever we needed to release. We turned our right hands palm up, with the stone in our palm, that this would be a prayer for us to receive whatever God needed us to receive. I invited them to join hands by placing their left hand over their neighbor's right so that each stone was tucked within the joining of hands, and then we offered words and phrases of blessing for you and for us all. It was lovely and a blessing to me. *Love love love*, I said as my blessing in the circle.

When we finished the blessing, I told them Scott would place the box in the hole and fill it in and that they were welcome to stay while he did this or to go back up to the packinghouse, where supper would soon appear. Everyone stayed, keeping silent as Scott completed the task with care. Suzanne and Jeff had picked some black-eyed Susans. When Scott was finished, I placed them on the earth that covered your ashes, secured them with a nearby stone, arranged several other stones in a circle atop the burial place, and laid my hands upon the earth in blessing.

We lingered there for a few minutes, taking in the late afternoon. Emile told me I had picked a beautiful spot, which warmed my heart.

—Wednesday, August 5, 2015—

In my session with Christianne last week, I found myself wondering whether I should lay aside doing an online retreat this Advent, and possibly Lent 2016. I had been assuming I would move forward as usual with those, so I was a little surprised to find the question surfacing for me. I've led four retreats since you died, and I always have questions about whether to do them, but this time it feels different, and I'm not clear what the invitation is.

This summer has held many gifts as I've allowed myself to move more slowly, work on the house, rest, move into your studio, spend lots of time with friends, read, ponder, pray. As the season (quickly) unfolds, I'm starting to wonder how it would be to let myself remain in this kind of rhythm for more than a season, to give myself upwards of a year to move at a different pace, particularly to write and make art without the pressure of a retreat. When the question came up for me with Christianne, I talked about my conviction that when we have a gift—writing or art, for instance—it seems we have a responsibility and a call to use it, and I wasn't clear how that could jibe with taking a break from the online retreats. She asked me, *How might those gifts be gifts for yourself right now?*

Christianne asks really good questions.

One of the things I wondered aloud to her was, *How would it be to let go of something I created with Gary?* Tears came as I asked. The question stirred much sorrow, and some fear.

There have been so many gifts with the retreats. Traveling through seasons with amazing folks. Having a compelling reason to write and make art. Continuing to work with and share your songs. How would it be to give this up for a time? But only for a time—perhaps for a year, and then returning.

I find myself wondering what could come in that time, what might show up if I set aside the retreats for a bit. I imagine painting in the studio, exploring and wandering without the immediate pressure to create for an audience.

—FRIDAY, AUGUST 21, 2015—

A fairly strange week.

The strangeness of the week has its roots in last weekend, when I did some more work on your studio. Last Saturday I swept and mopped the floor of the studio. I don't think that terrazzo floor has been professionally cleaned since the house was built in the '50s! The more I cleaned, the more frustrated I grew at the ground-in grime.

At any rate, it's good to get down to that layer of clearing and re-creating the studio, but also painful. Especially since beginning to work on the studio earlier this summer, it has felt like every molecule in my life and my body is being reordered.

In the process of preparing to sweep and mop the studio floor, I unplugged your mic and moved it and your mic stand into the guest room. I'd been doing some thinking about that part of your studio where your recording equipment is, and the stash of Louis L'Amour books that you were steadily working your way through. And your golf hat. I'd had some thought of clearing that space so I could use the top of the cabinet as part of my painting space, though I had decidedly mixed feelings about doing this. Moving the mic and stand felt like the first step.

That night, after I finally stopped mopping and mopping, I was exhausted. I had planned to do some work on/in the studio on Sunday but couldn't bear the thought. Then, when I was talking with friends after church on Sunday afternoon, I found tears coming as I tried to talk about the work I'd done in the studio the day before, about beginning to clear part of your space that felt uniquely personal to you. Your recording equipment. The place in the studio where you stood as you created your stunning songs. The place where you had books you were planning to read. I couldn't really speak it.

Later that night, it suddenly occurred to me—the significance not just of moving the mic and stand but of unplugging the mic in the first place, pulling the cord out of the recording device you used. *Unplugging*. Suddenly I was sitting on your hospital bed again, the day of your dying, watching the nurse unplug and remove all that had tethered you to this life. I wept and wept at the sudden connection between that unplugging and this one. With tears coursing down my face, I went to the guest room and picked up the mic stand. Carried it back to its place in your studio. Plugged it back in.

I am pained and glad to have made the connection. But it set the tone for a strange week. Not all bad strange, but not quite a typical week. And I've been so weary this week. So in the midst of the handful of commitments, I've mostly given myself a break and done a good bit of resting.

This makes me think of John O'Donohue, whose words are so often a solace in my grieving. I've been reading his book *Eternal Echoes*. In a chapter titled "Absence: Where Longing Still Lingers," he writes:

> Grief is the experience of finding yourself standing alone in the vacant space with all this torn emotional tissue protruding. In the rhythm of grieving, you learn to gather your given heart back to yourself again. This sore gathering takes time. You need great patience with your slow heart.

You need great patience with your slow heart. Yes. Perhaps this patience, this learning to move in the rhythm of my slow heart, is a way of entering into the kind of time that grief invites us into. Time that is fashioned of both *chronos* and *kairos*—sometimes crashing against each other, sometimes tugging at each other (and tugging me apart in the process), sometimes intertwining with an aching beauty and power and grace.

I think again of those words that came to me one morning as I woke shortly after your surgery: *slow rain, slow rain.* I had wondered if this was the kind of time you had already begun to move into, time no longer dominated and measured by *chronos.*

Perhaps this is my slow rain time. Time that is more like the kind of time you are experiencing now, if it can even be called *time.* I remember Lesley sharing words she sensed her mother saying to her sometime after her death: *Time is different here.*

I've been listening often to your music lately. It always comes as a grace when I can do this. It's been such a journey, regaining the ability to hear your voice, your songs; to enter into the joy and the sorrow of it. I am abidingly grateful that you and Greg recorded so many of your songs. Thank you and bless you, and him.

One of the songs I'm especially glad to have a recording of, from a concert you did, is "Albert Einstein and the Book of Hours." I've listened to it again a few times recently and am grateful to have not only the song but also your spoken-word piece that precedes it, which, like the song, you composed for *KATZ*:

> At the end of the day we only have our hands and our hearts and a dear few hours. The dark gathers steadily around us and sounds of the night fill us with foreboding, and, oh, if we could only have a little light, a little warmth. Look! We could build a fire. We have some kindling, a tinderbox. The black universe of exploding stars wheels above us and we only have our hands and our hearts and a dear few hours. And we only have this little fire to fend off the night. We are so small. Only dust, really. A tiny kernel in a tiny seed on a big wind.
>
> And this spilled jar of time is ever rushing to the table's edge and leaping, leaping out into the vastness. With our experience of each moment, each second of time, we set it free. We are the emancipators of captive time, the channel of its escape.
>
> I only know that this book of hours that is our lifelong reading, this liturgy of breathing in and breathing out, is our all but not *the* all. Within these borders we are bound for a time, for this time, for any time, for all time, but not beyond time. Beyond the ticking of our clocks we sense a living silence, and we know that we are surrounded by an unmeasured, uncreated *nowness*, that while we are involved in *having been* and in *waiting to be* there exists the *always is*; there exists the *I am* of which we are a part.
>
> Between these borders of birth and death is only a moment, only an island of time in the vast ocean of eternity. But while we are here we carry God's own breath of creation within us, and it is the breathing, the telling of our story, the casting of our spell that sustains us. We sing and enchant

the heavens and so are brought whole through the ordeal to
dance upon our own graves.

ALBERT EINSTEIN AND THE BOOK OF HOURS

When Albert opened the book of hours
He turned the pages one by one
And having read the book of hours
He closed the book when it was done

And maybe Albert Einstein was wide awake
And maybe Albert Einstein was dreaming
And rising from his slumbers for the morning's sake
He called up all his relatives to tell them he was home

He turned his eyes up to the heavens
And counted every star he found
And finding more than stars in the heavens
He turned his calculations round

And Jesus and the Buddha and Jelaluddin
Waving from the twinkling far
And fingering his pate with a bemused expression
Albert winds his timepiece and sets out on his way

Oh what we know and what we sense is real
These bear considering
And some reconsidering
This is my appeal

Albert Einstein and the book of hours
A sharing of mythologies
Parallel and convergent
They meet without apologies

And maybe Albert Einstein was wide awake
And maybe Albert Einstein was dreaming

And rising from his slumbers for the morning's sake
He called up all his relatives
His near and distant relatives
To notify his relatives
That finally he was home

Mercy, what an amazing piece. And so helpful to read the spoken-word part, especially when I've been doing a lot of thinking about time. Those lines, again:

Beyond the ticking of our clocks we sense a living silence, and we know that we are surrounded by an unmeasured, uncreated *nowness*, that while we are involved in *having been* and in *waiting to be* there exists the *always is*; there exists the *I am* of which we are a part.

Gorgeous, your notion that we are surrounded by *nowness*, by the *I am* that exists beneath and beyond past and future. And that we are part of this *I am*, this *nowness*.

How do you and I share in this *nowness* together? How do we abide with one another and know each other in this *I am*?

For the past four Sundays I've gone to the contemplative Celtic Eucharist at All Saints Episcopal in Winter Park. You and I had heard about this service, had planned to visit sometime. Christianne and Kirk regularly go to this service, along with some other friends. I had thought of it from time to time but, until recently, had chosen not to go because church is mostly too difficult right now, and because it's one of the places I miss you most. The Eucharist service has been a tender place, especially with its contemplative resonance with the Wellspring service, but it feels like a good place to be right now. Timely.

One of the main things that drew me to the service is that Eucharist had come up in conversations recently with both Maru and Christianne. That it came up with either one of them would have caused me to pay attention, so when it came up with both, it seemed especially important to pay attention. We talked about how Eucharist is a place where past, future, and present come together. Particularly given all the thinking I've been doing about time, it seemed like entering into this space, into this sacrament, might be important (and not just for that reason).

But what does this mean in the present? And how does the communion of saints participate in Eucharist, as Christian theology holds it does? When I show up at Eucharist, are you aware of it? Do you somehow share in it? Is it a place of meeting?

These questions hook into other questions I have about time, some of which have come up in conversation with Christianne. What is time for you—do you even experience some version of it, some form of it? Are you aware of time unfolding here, on this side of the veil? Do you know how I spend my days, how I am paging through this book of hours? If you're aware of it, do you have the ability to participate in it—for instance, in the synchronicities that so often feel as if they have come from you? Are you able, in your time, to sometimes intersect with mine? If you have entered fully into eternity, do you even have any comprehension of *chronos*?

I'm not going to Eucharist with the expectation that it will answer these questions for me. But I'm hoping that in joining in this sacrament, the grace of it will enter into me, will inhabit and bless those places that lie beneath and beyond logical comprehension. And that it will somehow be a thin place for us.

—SATURDAY, AUGUST 22, 2015—

All last night, I had "Albert Einstein and the Book of Hours" going through my head. It feels so fitting to have it on my mind as I ponder questions about time, eternity, heaven. The song greeted me as I woke today. Sweetheart, thank you for this amazing song, and for "The Art of Time," which I've also been listening to lately. Thank you for all your songs, for every song. I've remarked to Christianne how often a line from one of your songs will visit me, triggered by a situation or conversation or something I'm thinking about. It's tender but beautiful, and there is solace in it. Somehow seems like its own exercise in the art of time, how you have the power to offer consolation and companionship in the present with something you wrote in the past.

Your song, along with the noodling I've been doing about time and such, has gotten me thinking again about books of hours. One of the things I jotted down on an index card in the wee hours of this morning was, *What would a book of hours for eternity look like? Or is this what they already are?*

Earlier today I pulled out a couple of books about books of hours, both by Roger Wieck, and will be spending some time with them. I remember he talks about the book of hours as a portable cathedral—how the reader, wherever they were, could open its pages and enter into a space of prayer. I remember in my Soul of the Book class at the Guild, how I used this to talk about books as thin places. Windows onto eternity. And how some of the iconography in the books of hours, the design of the books, underscored this—for instance, in how the artists so often framed the scenes with archways, using these to play with concepts of time.

Last night I began to wonder how it might be to create a book of hours with you in mind. For a good while I've been pondering what I might do with your papers that have to do with the concerts you booked or were in the process of booking or hoping to book, papers that bear witness to a part of your vocation that was consuming and burdensome. It's tempting to want to burn them, to get rid of them for you in hopes that it will be a release for you (or at least for me). But I've been thinking about how I'd like to do something creative with those papers, something redemptive. Lately I've been thinking about making books with them. There are some design challenges, given that the papers aren't very heavy and crinkle easily, but I have some ideas about possibilities to try, and I need to get back into the studio to do some experimenting to see what I (we?) can come up with.

Book. The resonance of the word—booking a concert, making

a book—didn't hit me till writing the previous paragraph. Hm. Something to explore.

And of course I found myself thinking about a day, so long ago, when we were lying in your bed. I wish I could remember just what you said, but you were dreaming, I think, about spending the day together in bed—the morning, the afternoon, the evening. Whatever it was you were saying, it culminated in these words: *A book of hours in my bed.* I smiled in wonder; you didn't know about my fascination with books of hours. It gladdens my heart still—one of those beautiful serendipities that made it so clear you were the one for me.

So what kind of book of hours might we make together?

—Monday, August 24, 2015—

I've been thinking about memory the past few weeks. It began with a quote that came my way from Oliver Sacks: *We now know that memories are not fixed or frozen, like Proust's jars of preserves in a larder, but are transformed, disassembled, reassembled, and recategorized with every act of recollection.* Evidently that landed somewhere in my subconscious, because sometime during the following week, during my prayer time in the front studio one night, the quote came to the surface. It got me pondering in a new way what it is that remembering does and how it's part of my journey in grieving.

Specifically, I've been thinking about memory as a creative act, that perhaps in the disassembling and reassembling Sacks talks about, memory is generative. It's not just pondering and piecing together what happened in the past but also creating something for the future. I find myself with the sense that in remembering you, your story, and our life together, something new is being created, something that has a nearly tangible element to it—that it has structure, that it is a shelter, a new home between the worlds. That remembering is part of what we are doing together now. That when I remember, it's not so much a dwelling on the past as it is something that helps me, helps us, create a future.

I don't know if I'm right about that—I mean, I've long been aware that remembering has a future aspect to it, that we build our future in part from our memories—but this feels like a different shading, that memory is a place of meeting for us, a way of creating anew, both individually and together. Regardless of whether I'm right about this, it has come as a wonderfully comforting thought. When I do remember (which is constantly), this new awareness helps me feel a little less anguish and a little more hope. The re-membering isn't so much about aching over your absence (though there's still an awful plenty of that) but, in the midst of the aching, feeling like something abides and is becoming new. Being rebuilt, re-created, reassembled.

You—always so good at building things, I wrote on an index card a couple weeks ago as I was thinking about memory and creativity and generativity, this process of disassembling and reassembling and building anew. I have only to look around our home to see how good you were at building, including the custom-made pieces in my front studio and the beautiful, big table in your studio where I'm beginning to make a home. And the intangible things you were so good at building, not least of which has been our life together.

Memory and creativity, memory and generativity, memory and imagination, memory and dreaming, the art of memory, memory and Eucharist—these are just some of the trails I've been pursuing the past few weeks, turning up some interesting bits and pieces. I've talked some with Christianne about this, and those have been powerful conversations. A couple weeks ago, she asked, *How was remembering a part of your life with Gary? How might this continue now?*

Thought those were marvelous questions. Several weeks later, I wrote this on an index card: *Thinking about Christianne's questions re: memory. It is a form of intimacy—the memories that Gary and I have shared with each other, and that we have made together. Cf. his inscription in the Annie Proulx book.*

Intimacy came as you and I made memories together. Intimacy came also as we shared stories and memories of our lives before we met each other (was there ever such a time?)—as we (quickly) trusted each other with the sometimes difficult and painful memories we carried, many of which found healing in the telling and as we made our life together. It seems we have always been about memory. Even our first conversation felt like one we'd already been having a long time. From the start, we were remembering together.

About the inscription in the Annie Proulx book. You had a wonderful tradition, when I would get on a plane by myself (before we began to do so much traveling together for work), of sending me off with a book, a bag of Snickers, and a map of the place I was going to. (Mercy, Sweetheart—do I tell you often enough how marvelous you were/are?) When I headed to Philadelphia in 2002, you gave me *The Shipping News* (which we both loved; you said what she did in that novel was like jazz). This was your inscription:

My sweet Jan,

On your departure for Philadelphia, when we're apart, while you are away, I will find moments to stop and imagine what you are doing, who you are with, what hall or office or church you grace with your presence. And there will be times when an image of you comes unbidden to my mind—an intimate moment will steal my breath, your laugh or sweet smile, a tender, understanding word, will bless my day.
    I love you deeply and with all my heart.

Your Sweetheart,
Gary

I love how, in the wondrous words in your inscription, memory and imagination come together; and intimacy, too, as something you specifically name. And your heart. Your amazing heart. It prompts me to wonder what inspiration and guidance there might be for me in these words—how you intertwine memory and imagination and intimacy and heart. How might I—how might we—continue to do this now?

I am thinking also of memories as living tissue, something that binds us together.

The shelter of story.

All this thinking about memory has given me cause to recall and revisit those words that Lewis Carroll wrote in *Through the Looking-Glass*, where the White Queen says to Alice, *It's a poor sort of memory that only works backwards*. Feeling the truth of this in a new way. Memory as something that helps make it possible for us to move forward, live forward, build forward, create forward.

Memories as seeds. Remembering Clarissa Pinkola Estés's words that you wrote down from her talk that we heard in Washington—the story about the seeds in the wounds of the wall—the scrap of paper on which you wrote her words, *The story's not over.*

I remember how glad I was to come across that small scrap after you died and to be reminded of those words.

What seeds lie in the wounds in our wall? What seeds can we put there? What stories might they yet hold?

Thinking about memory is part of what propelled me toward the contemplative Eucharist service at All Saints—the sacrament of the table as a place of memory that calls us not only to remember and give thanks for what God has done for us in the past but also to imagine and receive sustenance for what God will yet bring about in and through us. How Christ remakes us in this. Re-members us. Enables us to put the pieces together anew.

As I was doing some poking around online about memory and Eucharist, these words by Pierre Teilhard de Chardin came up, from *The Divine Milieu*:

> When the priest says the words *Hoc est corpus meum* [*This is my body*], his words fall directly on to the bread and directly

transform it into the individual reality of Christ. But the great sacramental operation does not cease at that local and momentary event.... These different acts are only the diversely central points in which the continuity of a unique act is split up and fixed, in space and time, for our experience. In fact, from the beginning of the Messianic preparation, up till the Parousia, passing through the historic manifestation of Jesus and the phases of growth of his Church, a single event has been developing in the world: the Incarnation, realised, in each individual, through the Eucharist.

All the communions of a life-time are one communion.

All the communions of all men now living are one communion.

All the communions of all men, present, past and future, are one communion.

This feels like part of the answer to my question about how you are in the Eucharist, particularly if you are unbound by time. (Are you unbound by time?) I'm drawn to the notion that all Communions—present, past, future—are one Communion. If this is true, then somehow all the Communions we shared—I think particularly of the Wellspring service—are present in the Eucharist at All Saints and that you are somehow participating in this in a way beyond my understanding. That we are sharing in that meal, that sacrament, together, both receiving the grace and sustenance of it. *Real presence.* I think of this not only in relation to what Christ does in Eucharist, how he is present in the sacrament, but how you might be present as well.

Part of what feels so reassuring about thinking of memory as generative is that it means when I remember our life together, I'm not just remembering. I have tended to think there were two possibilities with respect to my experience of you now: that you abide or that you are present only as a memory. I have denigrated memory a bit, with respect to your death—grateful beyond measure for the memories we share but not thinking of the act of memory as something that might point toward the possibility that you abide. I still hold questions, of course, about whether you abide in a form that I will see and know one day, when my own life here is done. Yet the possibility that memory is generative, that it is something we share, that it is creating something new and not simply rehashing the past: this is hopeful. Hopeful, too, that the act and art of remembering might deepen our knowing of one another—might continue to cultivate intimacy between us.

Memory as one of the ways you actively abide.

Memory itself as having a sacramental quality. Something of this came up with Christianne, in that same conversation where she asked how remembering was part of our life together. She brought up Eucharist—how it intertwines the tangible and intangible, how this is part of what a sacrament does. (*A visible sign of an invisible grace*, as the saying goes.) She talked about how I am doing this in my life now—intertwining (or noticing the intertwining of) the tangible and intangible. Making visible what is invisible.

So Eucharist at All Saints (All Saints! how apt) seems like a good place to be right now, for many reasons, not least of which is that it's a place to let the threads of memory, sacrament, and grace gather and see what comes.

Memory like honey, storing away the sweetness. Wrote that on an index card a couple weeks ago.

—WEDNESDAY, AUGUST 26, 2015—

I realized I haven't written here about the dream of the ladder.

Sometime last year, I had a dream in which you and I were at the Evinston house, as it looked when I was growing up. We were in the front bedroom that was, at different times, my bedroom or Sally's. You and I were on a ladder—a straight ladder—with you on one side, me on the other. We were working to stay balanced on the ladder and were doing a sort of dancing, gymnastics-y kind of thing, moving up and sort of sliding down the ladder.

In the dream I had a very physical sensation of learning how to do this—of coming into balance and being able to move with

greater ease. I loved the sensation of learning this, of being able to do it. You were already good at it—you already knew this choreography, this art, and were helping me learn how to balance and move with you.

I think this is my favorite dream I've had of you since you died. I love the image of being on the ladder with you and learning to balance and move with you with grace. Such resonance with the ladder image, especially with the story of Jacob that we have so loved, with his vision of the liminal ladder stretched between heaven and earth, with angels ascending and descending. Perhaps you have been learning from the angels.

The dream prompted me to remember a charcoal drawing I had done years earlier, when I was first starting to experiment with charcoal (for the art for Peter Storey's book). I did a small, spare drawing of a ladder. It was a one-off drawing, pretty unlike anything else I'd done. After the dream, I went searching for the drawing. I looked through years' worth of art stuff and finally, after quite a bit of looking, found it stuck in a pad of drawing paper in a stack of drawing tablets I had already gone through.

I was so glad to finally find the drawing that I hadn't seen since before we moved me out of the Maitland apartment. Particularly since it was a one-off kind of drawing, it felt a little like a message to myself from years ago—or perhaps not so much a message as a bit of solace. A point of connection across time, between my younger and present self, between my waking and dreaming self, and between you and me. I put the drawing in your studio.

The dream of the ladder isn't the only dream that has conveyed a sense that you've learned how to do something—that you're further along in this process—and that you want to help me. Some months ago, I dreamed you and I were in Gainesville. You were driving. We had been heading north on I think Main Street, in south Gainesville, then turned around and backtracked south. We were looking for a Comfort Inn. Suddenly I saw it on the left and said, *There it is! Turn here!* You were already on it, and, in your beautifully calm and reassuring way, you told me, *Don't worry; I've got this.*

Looking for comfort. And you've already found it, intent on providing it for me. Taking care of me in the lovely way you always have.

Eucharist came up in conversation with Maru last month. We were talking about memory, time, and Eucharist, and she said, *Eucharist is happening in the now that now is.* She spoke of memory as a portal, the gates of encounter. *Memory is like an icon,* she said. *We can leave it as a picture on a wall or use it as a portal of presence.*

Feeling our way into the is-ness, I also wrote down from that conversation. Not certain whether Maru was talking about memory or Eucharist, but I think it can apply to both. Both memory and Eucharist are ways to enter into time in its present sense—time as presence. *Feeling our way into the is-ness*—this so resonates with your prelude to "Albert Einstein and the Book of Hours."

I love this, too, from your prelude:

Between these borders of birth and death is only a moment, only an island of time in the vast ocean of eternity. But while we are here we carry God's own breath of creation within us, and it is the breathing, the telling of our story, the casting of our spell that sustains us. We sing and enchant the heavens and so are brought whole through the ordeal to dance upon our own graves.

Oh, my love. My brilliant sweetheart. How you must be enchanting the heavens! I pray you know yourself brought whole through the ordeal, dancing upon your own grave, beautiful and defiant and singing at the top of your lungs.

In our conversation last month, Maru and I talked also about absence; I probably shared some of John O'Donohue's thinking about absence being the sister of presence. *Sacred absence*, Maru said along the way, *is more like sacred spaciousness. It houses a living heartbeat.*

I first heard John O'Donohue talk about absence and presence in his wonderful *Pilgrimage* DVD that Christianne loaned me not long before I left for Ireland in May. It was just a passing comment, as I recall—*Absence is the sister of presence.* It seized my attention, my imagination. I carried it with me to Ireland and thought about it often. I began to think about absence as an art, a practice—that there is something nearly tangible about absence, that even in the bareness of it and in the ache that so often accompanies absence, there is some—for lack of a better word—*energy* to it—an essence, a vibration; that the shape and contour of absence bear witness to something that abides. *A living heartbeat*, as Maru put it. I think again of the day you died and the words of the nurse who told me, *His heart beats in you now.*

While I was traveling with the gang in Ireland this summer, we found a wondrous bookstore in Galway City called Charlie Byrne's Bookshop. My favorite bookstore in Ireland. That is saying something—we found some lovely bookstores! A number of rooms to wander through. The group had a good browse there, and I stayed on and had them swing back by when they were ready to leave the city. I found a book called *Walking on the Pastures of Wonder*, published just this year, in which a radio producer named John Quinn gathered together a number of John O'Donohue's talks. There's a beautiful chapter called "Absence." Here are some excerpts that especially struck me and bear more contemplating:

> The opposite of presence is not absence, but vacancy. Vacancy is a neutral, indifferent, inane, blank kind of space, whereas absence has real energy; it has vitality in it, and it is infused with longing. . . .
>
> . . . There is a place where our vanished days secretly gather. Memory, as a kingdom, is full of the ruins of presence. . . . Memory is the place where absence is transfigured and where our time in the world is secretly held for

us.... Memory keeps presence alive and is always bringing out of what seemed to be absent new forms of presence.

Sometime after I returned home from Ireland, I ordered John's book *Eternal Echoes*, which also has a chapter on absence ("Where Longing Still Lingers"). He says many of the same things about absence, but he adds this:

> The ebb and flow of presence and absence is the current of our lives; each of them configures our time and space in the world. Yet there is a force that pervades both presence and absence: this is spirit. There is nowhere to locate spirit and neither can it be subtracted from anything. Spirit is everywhere. Spirit is in everything. By nature and definition, spirit can never be absent. Consequently, all space is spiritual space, and all time is secret eternity. All absence is full of hidden presence.

All time is secret eternity. Yes. Perhaps this is part of what connects *chronos* and *kairos* and what connects you and me—that however it manifests, all time is, as John writes, secret eternity.

Grateful for his image of the ebb and flow of presence and absence as the current of our lives. His words return me to the dream of floating down the river with you, belly to belly.

My writing has been interspersed with other things this evening, including a phone visit with Mom and Dad. Now the night is far gone. Time to get ready for bed. Please meet me in the dreaming, Sweetheart; please be with me in that current, with all its absence and all its presence.

—MONDAY, SEPTEMBER 7, 2015—
Gainesville

Had a beautiful final evening on Tybee yesterday with the Candler chicks. At the end of dinner, I pulled out one of the stones with *beloved* inscribed on it, from the day we buried your ashes. I had told the group about the stones and that I had several extras I was planning to leave at some significant places. I asked them to pass around the stone and welcomed them to say something brief if they wished, or simply to pass it in silence. Each person said something beautiful. I can hardly recall their words now, but they came as a gift.

Before passing around the stone, I had dampened it with water to bring out *beloved*; it was one of a few stones that were a little mottled and not inscribed very deeply, so it's hard to see the letters unless the stone is just a little damp. Linda noticed that the water was drying in a way that revealed the word as *be loved*.

I remember that Lesley said, *You were so much more together, but you are not less than you were now.*

Dorri said something about loving you because of how much you loved me.

Then we walked down to the beach. As it happened, it was sunset, and it was gorgeous. We walked to the water, and with my feet in the surf, I threw the *beloved* stone out into the river. We stood there for a long while, talking and being quiet and watching the stunning setting of the sun. I shared lines from your song "Hymn of the Stone":

> All I am is a stone in the river
> At rest in the river
> As still as a stone
> All I am is a stone in the river
> I am not the river
> I am ever and only a stone

With my heel I traced a big heart in the sand.

Without even having a complete idea of just how I wanted it to go (and probably precisely because I didn't have a complete idea), the evening was beautiful and perfect. So very grateful.

I've been continuing to think about memory and what remembering does in grieving. Sometime this summer, during my nighttime prayer in the front studio, I found myself praying: *I remember, I remember, I remember.* Repeating it again and again in my head, my heart.

All of a sudden it occurred to me to wonder, *Do you pray this for me?* I've had that sensation several times since your death—praying something and then suddenly having the feeling that what I'm praying for, you might be praying for me. It came as a gorgeous gift—that you might be wanting me to know that you remember me, that you remember us. It touches on those questions I've carried: *Does he remember me? Does he remember our life, does he think of me still, does he know me?* Though I still don't know the answers to such questions, I love receiving the hints and glimmers that suggest the answer to those questions is *yes.*

PART SIX
The Room Where the Books Begin

BETWEEN

I could not
have dreamed it
so vast—

this place we meet
in the scar between
the worlds.

A little over a month ago, in my evening prayer time in the front studio, a scene came to me as I was praying. I had been thinking of the image of the bowls of incense from Revelation 5. In the scene, you and I were in a space something like one of the hallways in the place where I stayed in Kenmare, in Ireland, earlier this year. It is, in real life, a soothingly shadowed space with occasional lighting along the way. I was walking with you down the hallway, following a bit behind you. You were carrying a luminous bowl of incense.

I followed you into a room where there was a small, narrow table. You placed the bowl on the table, and we sat across from each other. There was a book already there. You opened the book. The pages appeared blank. You passed your hand across a page, and wonders appeared. Something like in an illuminated manuscript, though I had a sense that some of what appeared as you passed your hand across each page was in motion—that it was not fixed, not bound. I didn't have a sense of what the images contained. I knew only that you were showing me marvels, wonders—things that lay ahead.

I scribbled some notes about the scene on an index card that night, and at the end I wrote this: *The book as a place of meeting.*

Place of meeting refers to the book in this imagined scene—that the book you showed me, which seemed empty but held wonders beneath your hand, is a place where you and I can meet. It is a place of revelation. There is solace there.

The book as a place of meeting refers also, I think, to ideas I've had about what to do with some of the pages you left behind—the administrative stuff having to do with booking concerts. I want to redeem those pages. So I've had the notion of somehow turning them into books. I'm not sure how to do this and have let myself get pretty stalled out with it because of my lack of knowing. But it feels like perhaps time to do more experimenting, to put this studio—our studio—to use and see what comes.

I've had the notion for some time of creating books with blank pages—perhaps even letting them remain blank for a time. (Did a little experimenting a while back with painting the pages white.) Perhaps to see what wonders will come from the empty pages. Just at the time I began thinking about creating books with empty pages, I came across this poem by Rumi:

> I hear nothing in my ear
> but your voice. Heart has
>
> plundered mind of all its
> eloquence. Love writes a
>
> transparent calligraphy, so
> on the empty page my soul
>
> can read and recollect.

Loved coming across that image; love it still, with its invitation to know the presence of love in an empty page.

Absence and presence.

What might I find in making empty pages from the pages you left behind? What might find its way to those pages? What might arise from them? How might we meet one another there, eyes open to the wonders?

—SUNDAY, SEPTEMBER 20, 2015—

In my prayer time last night, after writing here, I found myself thinking about the book of blessings I've been working on, and it occurred to me that it too could be a book that is a meeting place. Is already a meeting place, in fact, given that you saw every blessing before I sent it into the world, often working through word choices with me. You were in each blessing. And we had talked so much about a book of blessings; I had even printed out all the blessings not so long before you went into the hospital and had wanted to have another conversation with you after doing that, but somehow, in all the coming and going, we didn't do that. But you are still so much a part of the book—which has both drawn me toward the project and also daunted me at times.

So it was helpful, last night, to think of the book of blessings as a place of meeting—perhaps even that it is part of the book of wonders you were showing me in the scene I wrote about last night. In that vein, I pray that you will help show me the way forward with the book and that you will stir up the energy, focus, grace, and anything else I need in order to work on this book. Please bless me as I work on it. Please meet me there.

—Monday, November 2, 2015—

I have been pretty well consumed the past few weeks—I can't remember now how long, maybe upwards of a month now—with completing the book of blessings, which I'm calling *Circle of Grace*. Just looked back at what I wrote in my last entry, near the end of September, about the book as a meeting place. It has felt like that. I think it was shortly after writing that that I returned to work on the book, intently and intensively.

I spent much of the past week in Gainesville finishing the book. It felt fitting to be completing the book as Halloween became All Saints.

So often during the past few weeks, when I have come to the surface after a stretch of working on the book, I have had the sensation that I've been with you. It has come as a great comfort and has underscored my sense about the book—books generally and this book of blessings specifically—as a place of meeting, a place where I can know you. I don't even quite know what that means, but I sense the truth of it.

What a journey this book of blessings has been. I feel so many things as I prepare to release it. You have been such a part of it, with having seen and provided insight into most of the blessings before I posted them at The Painted Prayerbook and with all the conversations we had about this book. It feels both sad and immeasurably sweet to be about to release it. Even as I know you are such a part of it, it is a keen sorrow not to have you here, in the flesh, as it makes its way into the world.

In the past few weeks I've been sensing a recommitment to be a person who creates books. That was perhaps my earliest call, and it has seemed strange to me that I've released so few books in the past fifteen years, though I am very aware those years have held other book-like things, or things that will eventually make their way into books—the online retreats, the work I've done on my blogs—all of which you have been such a part. This feels like a time for focusing on creating books, and the book of blessings seems a very fitting place to renew that commitment.

So much more to say, but for tonight, simply this: how much I love you, how much I miss you, how much I want to know you still. On this Feast of All Souls, my soul is so grateful for yours. Stay with me, Sweetheart. Meet me in the book-making and in every place possible.

—Wednesday, December 2, 2015—

Two years today. A moment and an eternity.

I just returned home today from being in Gainesville for Thanksgiving. I was grateful to begin this day at Mom and Dad's; sweet conversations with both of them. Grateful also to have tea at Infusion with Christianne shortly after arriving home this afternoon. So very thankful for her. And, as I might have said here before, am suspicious you had a hand in sending her to me. If so, thank you. A million times over.

So much I want to write here. And so weary tonight. I am continuing to keep index cards, wanting to remember, saving them for the time I will return here with more intention.

Thank you for helping me make it through another year, another day, another moment. I love you and bless you this night and always, Sweetheart.

—Sunday, December 13, 2015—

Well, here we are, deep into Advent. With deciding not to do the Advent retreat this year, and with having finished and released the book of blessings and made it through the release party last weekend, I am having a new experience: finding some space to breathe and to move through the season with less of a plan or agenda.

In this space, in this different kind of Advent rhythm, some questions specific to the season have come to the surface. Questions like, *Are the dead aware of the liturgical seasons? How might I know you in this season? Is there some particular way you might want to reveal yourself in Advent? Is there some way I might reveal myself to you in this season? Are there gifts we can still exchange?*

These have been good questions to take into prayer, though so far the glimmers of answers have been few.

In my quiet time in the front studio several nights ago, praying about these things, I was visited by a wave of ideas for an article or reflection about grief and Advent, out of my own keen need for something more than "managing" my grief in this season (which is what most folks who write about grief and the holidays write about).

I made lots of notes and am feeling energy for writing about this—about how the stories and images of this season offer such richness and have something to speak into our grief. The interplay of heaven and earth that we see in the texts for Advent and Christmas, the offering and receiving of sanctuary (Mary and Elizabeth), creativity as an antidote to the ways grief can gut our imaginations (Mary's Magnificat), and more.

This feels like part of the work I'm being called to now—to be present to my own grief with the eye and heart and tools of a writer, a poet, an artist, both for my own solace and that of others. *Solace* in much the sense that David Whyte writes about it—*the art of asking the beautiful question.*

And what does solace look like in Advent? Some beautiful questions have come my way in this season; what do I do with them?

A couple of nights ago, there in the prayer corner of my front studio, I had such a meltdown as I pondered these questions. I had sensed the meltdown coming. I think that, in part, a lot was catching up with me—being done with the book of blessings, feeling the effects of all that went into the book celebration (which involved giving my first talk since your death, other than the last Wellspring service), and being in the thick of the holidays. I had gone to Barnes & Noble that morning for a few things that were part of my thank-you gifts to those who helped at the book celebration. I've been there just a few times since you died, and it still is a place of tenderness for me; that was only more true with its being the holidays.

Going into that prayer time a couple nights ago, I was angry—had been aware of that off and on during the day. When the tears finally came, they were filled with rage and sorrow and confusion and lingering incredulity that you are gone. It still feels so wrong and stupid that you have died, so utterly absurd.

I don't know what to do with all that except to be present to it. To let it be part of my prayer. I felt wiped out afterward. I have let myself move slowly this weekend and stay with the questions.

One thing that glimmered through the meltdown was this. In the thick of Advent, I was feeling a particularly keen ache and longing that night—for what, I'm not entirely sure, but something to do with yearning to know you, to have some inkling from you of what that knowing means in this season.

A piece of the meltdown—one of the many things it was about—was that I didn't have a sense of what it means to know you in this season. It felt like one of those times I was on the edge of something, when an insight or image or question or *something* was about to show up and provide what I needed—solace or illumination or some other gift. I didn't sense its arrival that night or that it was on its way. It just felt like lots of meltdown with no meaning.

But—and this is what I was heading toward at the beginning of the previous paragraph—one thing that came was this: aware of my aching, my longing, my yearning, I began to wonder if what I was feeling—that keen yearning—was something of what you were feeling for me, or alongside me. As I've written before, this kind of

sensation has happened a few times in prayer, when I've been praying about something that has intense feeling or force connected
with it, and I find myself wondering, *Are you praying this for me? Is
this something you desire for me?*

I don't know if that's true, if that's possible, but I notice it when
it happens. And I wonder if that's a place of connection, and perhaps a way you continue to tend my soul and my heart.

A night or two before that—I think it was one of the first nights I'd
gone into the studio to pray during Advent—an image came: you
giving me a sparrow for a heart. A sparrow with all the resonance of
the sparrow that appears in Psalm 84: a sparrow that makes its nest,
its home, in the presence of God. How might that space—part of
that space—be in my own heart? And what does this mean for me?
It was a lovely response to my question about whether there are
gifts you and I can still give each other.

What might I give you?

Last night I dreamed of you. It had been a while since you'd
appeared in my dreaming, at least in my remembering. (That's part
of what I pray—not only that you will meet me in the dreaming,
but also that I will remember when I dream of you.) We had spread
out a quilt or a blanket in a field. You were on the blanket, and
to get near you, I rolled over and over a few times, laughing as I
landed beside you. We exchanged gifts. I don't recall what the gifts
were, only that my gift for you was, I think, something I'd wrapped
around a tube, like a shortened version of one of the mailing tubes
I use to ship my art prints. I was concerned that whatever it was—
fabric, perhaps, but more likely paper—would crinkle.

I would love to know what gifts we gave each other in the
dream.

So what do you think about Advent, Sweetheart? Do you think
of Advent at all? Are you aware of the turning of time here and
what season we are in?

Last night, in my praying, it occurred to me that if you know anything of me still, if you have any awareness of what my life is like now, then surely you must know it's Advent, as it is so present in my mind and heart. And if you are indeed aware of this season, is there something we might know of one another in these days, some particular invitation this time of year holds for us?

It feels like time to head back into the studio with that question.

Soon after I lit the candle in my prayer corner, I decided to listen to one of your tapes—one of the eight cassettes with the informal recordings you made as you worked on songs. I listened to one or two a few months ago. I pulled out the second one, not sure if I had listened to it already. After beginning to play it, I realized I had but decided to keep listening.

It occurred to me this could be part of my Advent practice, part of my gift to you in this season: to listen to you. I often listen to you; thankfully, I'm able to listen to your songs more than I used to be able to, and I often play one of your CDs when I'm in the car. This week, I listened to your *Songmaker's Christmas* CD for the first time since your death. I had to skip past "How Will I Celebrate This Christmas?"

When I talk about listening to you as part of the gift, I mean listening to your music during my prayer time, making my way through the rest of the tapes during this season. In my praying and listening tonight, I thought about what an extraordinary privilege it has been to listen to you, to be your audience. To be someone who heard you well. I want to keep doing this, in whatever way I can.

Listening to you tonight, I thought of a poem I read a few months ago in Marie Ponsot's collection *The Bird Catcher*. One poem that particularly tugged at my heart and imagination is called "Even," where she writes:

Eve came to invent us
            invent audience
taking in hearing
she came to hear him:
            sponsa
            respondens

the birth of responsible life

He would hear her
she would be there to hear

She came to hear him. That so struck me. Eve as inventing audience.

He would hear her / she would be there to hear. How heard I was by you. How I loved hearing you and being your audience.

I love it still.

So this will be part of my Advent practice. Hearing you. Listening. Praying there will be an exchange of gifts in this.

Listening to you tonight, I found myself also thinking this: Song was (is?) the substance and essence of who you were (are?). Song and love, which perhaps are the same thing in you.

And, finally, this: That you know something about Advent that I don't. That because of where you are and what you now see and know, you not only know and are aware of this season, but you know something wondrous about it that perhaps I have yet to see and know.

Whatever it is, might I get a glimpse of it in this season? Might I somehow see it through your eyes, hear it through your hearing, your singing?

—SATURDAY, JANUARY 30, 2016—

Today I made a labyrinth in our home.

I've had labyrinths on my mind of late. It began during Advent, as I was praying in the front studio one night. I haven't walked a labyrinth since sometime before you died—the last one was the Celtic triple spiral labyrinth at the Guild. I love that labyrinth made of stones, overlooking the river. I remember candlelit labyrinth walks, the community walking together, you accompanying us on guitar.

During that Advent prayer time, an image of a labyrinth came to mind. This is what I jotted down: *Treading a labyrinth whose path only we have ever walked. Yet somehow it is ancient. We make the path with our walking, with our weeping, with our dancing. This labyrinth extends into (at least) four dimensions, including time. It is a space where we can ask questions and hold them as we walk. The heart as a labyrinth.*

The labyrinth has stayed with me, though it is more fluid than fixed. It varies, what the labyrinth is made of. Sometimes I have a sense you and I are treading the same path but you are walking the path from beneath—that our feet tread opposite sides of the path.

I'm drawn to that initial sense I had that we are making the path as we go but that somehow there is something ancient about it.

Another night, these thoughts:

We are in the studio—the one that's established itself in my imagination, the one I think of as the room where the books begin. We are sitting at a table. Christ is at the table with us—this is the first time I've seen him there—and he is looking smug. This is both annoying and somehow endearing. Mostly annoying. I sense he's looking smug over the fact that we found each other, that he led us to each other.

As he sits there, he places his hands near his heart. Pages begin to spiral out from his heart, encompassing us.

The next night, during my prayer time, this:

You and I are navigating the labyrinth made by the pages (the ones spiraling out from Christ's heart)—but we are also somehow making the pages by what we are each creating.

And as we create these pages, we are also creating the labyrinth that we are walking—the labyrinth that is both new and ancient.

And this, the following night:

I have a sense that the labyrinth is sometimes like a nest—intricate, intertwining, many-layered. Makes me think of the words you once wrote on an index card about how life should be a series of adventures launched from a secure base. Labyrinth: travel, exploration. Nest: security, home.

The labyrinth stuck with me. I found myself wishing there were a labyrinth nearby that I could walk. I've also been having a hankering for a labyrinth that is something other than two-dimensional. I've felt kind of stuck, not knowing what to do.

The night of January 4, I wrote this during my prayer time: *The trail I am on that has led me to the work of folks such as Tess Gallagher, Raymond Carver, Christian Wiman, N. T. Wright, Paula Gooder—this is a way of walking this labyrinth with Gary.*

I'm on quite a reading trail. This feels like something of a labyrinth in itself—that the reading is part of the labyrinth we are creating together.

That night, I had this dream:

I am in a place that I'm familiar with in the dream (I don't recognize it in my waking life). It feels a bit like a lovely hotel or a country home. I'm up on the second floor, looking out from a spot where there's a bank of windows. For the first time, I see the remains of a labyrinth. I hadn't been able to see it previously from the ground level, but from the second floor, it's visible.

I go downstairs to explore the labyrinth. It is an old labyrinth, made of stone. Much of it is worn away, but this intrigues me rather than bothers me. I have to work at finding the path. I am relieved to have found this labyrinth.

In the dream, I'm aware that, as in waking life, I've been wanting to walk a labyrinth, and that it's been a long time.

As I begin walking, trying to find the path, I'm aware of people nearby. They're talking about rebuilding the labyrinth. I think that's fine, but I am happy with the labyrinth as it is.

I loved this dream. It was a wondrous sensation to find a labyrinth in a place I thought I knew.

I found myself wishing there was a way to create a labyrinth in our home, but that didn't seem feasible, as there's no single room that could hold a decent-sized labyrinth. I'm not drawn to the small canvas labyrinths designed for homes and offices; a neat idea, but I haven't seen one I like. I thought about alternate materials—was there something I could use to create a labyrinth in our home?

Yesterday afternoon I brought in a box of stones from the garage—the ones left over from when I had the stones engraved with *beloved* for the day we buried your ashes. I rolled the big table in our studio to one side and laid out a spiral with those stones. I needed a few more and used the ones you had saved in a small glass—stones we used in our retreats. I spent some time walking the stone spiral with your Advent guitar meditations playing.

Today, in the late afternoon, I finished the labyrinth. Stones now stretch from our studio down the hallway and spiral through the studio and family room. I walked the full labyrinth tonight—three times slowly; took me close to an hour—and listened to some of your music for the Lenten retreat as I walked.

The labyrinth is, loosely, a Celtic triple spiral. It feels resonant with the imaginings I've had about our labyrinth (that struck me as I wrote it, *our labyrinth*), that it's both ancient and new. It feels resonant also with my dream, that it appeared in a place I was familiar with. I can't think of anything that's more familiar than our home. Though I created the labyrinth rather than finding it in the way I did in the dream, there still felt like an element of discovery—figuring out how to create a labyrinth within the space of our home and using materials we already had.

I've been thinking about other materials I can create the labyrinth from. The next thing I want to tackle is creating a labyrinth that's a book or a book that's a labyrinth. Am thinking about a small folding book—or, rather, lots of little books that can be laid out together in a similar Celtic spiral pattern. Books that I'll make. Had already had on my mind for quite some time that I wanted to make books as part of this grieving path. Now have an idea where to begin and am eager to get started. Did go to my paper shelves this evening to see what I have on hand; found a half dozen or so sheets of Rives BFK paper, which will be great for this. Will begin by cutting strips of the paper and folding the strips into small accordion books. Then will begin to fill the pages. So many ideas; so many directions I want to explore. And I do want it to be an exploration—to go in with as little agenda as possible, except to make, to create, to fashion and follow some lines and see where they take me.

Several times recently I've revisited a book I made at the Guild one year while teaching a Soul of the Book class. I created it from a meandering book form Gilly gave me, where I played with the text of a poem ("The Layers" by Stanley Kunitz, sent to me by Mary as I was leaving for the Guild). Had much fun with that. It's one of my inspirations for the labyrinth book I want to make, to spend some time at the table in our studio, pen and ink at hand, making marks and lines and patterns on paper, then cutting up the pieces and gluing them into my (our?) labyrinth book. And words. Many words. But lots of space too, like in the meandering book I made at the Guild. Room to breathe.

—THURSDAY, JUNE 9, 2016—
Kenmare, Ireland

After a long stretch away from these pages (more than four months since my last entry), I've landed in Ireland, where I'm working on a new book of blessings. Came here with a binder of blessings I had gathered together several months ago—candidates for this next book, which will include blessings for grief, struggle, and hope.

Christianne spent some time with the candidates before I left, and we had a really helpful conversation.

You are already so much a part of this book, which, as previously, makes it both wondrous and tender to work on. I think I learned some things about navigating that tension as I worked on *Circle of Grace* and am perhaps feeling it slightly less keenly with this new book so far, but that dynamic certainly is still present, particularly given the themes of this book.

At any rate, on Monday I spent some time downstairs after breakfast, beginning to go through the blessings I've gathered together for this book, doing some reorganizing, and making notes for the introduction.

I headed out to lunch at Jam, which has become a semi-regular lunch spot. I had been there for a bit and was nearly finished with my lunch when a couple of fellows who seemed to be father and son sat at the table next to me. I had taken my binder of blessings with me and was continuing to go through them (it was the first time I'd taken the blessings into town with me), and after a while, the father asked if I was working on a collection of my poems or someone else's.

It turned out he was the poet and writer John W. Sexton. His question led to an intriguing conversation. It was a real pleasure to meet both him and his son. As they were about to leave, I commented on the serendipity of meeting. *Synchronicity City*, he said. *It's where I live.*

I thought of how fond you and I have been of synchronicity and how frequently we noticed it and spoke of it. (*God winking*, you called it.) I am grateful for the spirit of synchronicity that continues in my life, that persists in weaving through my days. I love those synchronicities, love how frequently they've happened with books—how fitting this is to us, who have so loved books.

The space where I'm doing most of my writing here is the place with the hallway that, some months after I was last in Ireland, led my imagination into the space I've written about: the room where the books begin. I was curious to see how it would be to visit it again and whether it would be as I remembered it.

The first time I opened the door onto the hallway on this trip, it was comforting to find it was much as I recalled: a darkened hallway, dotted with tea lights along the way.

It's lovely to pass through this hallway into the place where I am writing. I'm in a far corner where two large glass walls meet to my right. To my left, there's a wall with water falling down it. Hoping its flow will help inspire the rhythm of my words.

I have been planning to work primarily on the new book of blessings while here and have made some progress with that, between spending time with the existing blessings and beginning to write new ones. But yesterday I found myself not in much of a mood to work on new blessings and am in a similar space today. I knew, as I prepared for this trip, that I would need to hold my expectations loosely, and I brought several things I could work on. But this is one of those times, as I encounter so often in grieving, where I find myself asking, *Is this a place where I need to let go or to stretch myself?*

Yesterday, as I carried that question, I worked on the book from a different direction. This included spending time here, writing in these pages and going through some months' worth of my writing to you, partly to see what territory I've traveled and partly to see if there were words among these pages that might inspire blessings. I did pull out a few things and will likely do more of that over the next day or two. I began today's work by reading the writing I had done here over the last few months. It was not much, but I was glad for what I had managed to set down on these pages, to capture some of what had unfolded.

A couple of weeks before I left on this trip, I found myself thinking about the Faddan More Psalter and the chat I had last year with the Keeper of Manuscripts in the Old Library at Trinity College Dublin. I began to wonder, *What is the book I need to dig up in Ireland?* This question, when it came to the surface, was a gift, and I have carried it here with me.

I don't know that the book I need to dig up here is anything other than this new book of blessings. But it's been a good question to carry, to keep my heart and mind open to what might want to show up beyond what I've brought with me.

I've begun to wonder if this time here might be, at least in part, about excavation—that this is not necessarily a time for producing polished pieces (though I'm still drawn to the idea of leaving Ireland with a fistful of new blessings) but focusing on opening my heart and brain and being to whatever wants to present itself and working to get it down on the page, no matter how messy it might be. Like the psalter: bog-drenched and in fragments, but already bearing treasure.

I'm keenly aware of how long it's been since I've written, and while I don't feel drawn to dwell on that—I'd like these entries to consist of more than *Dang, look at how long it's been since I've last written here*—I do want to jot down a couple of thoughts.

Over the past months, I've thought a lot about these pages, aware that I was feeling drawn to write here and also resistant to it. I think in part this was because so much has been stirring in the past months—in my heart and mind and soul, in prayer, in conversation—and with such intensity, it felt overwhelming (especially in a time when I've felt so little energy) to try and capture any of it, though I've continued to make notes on my index cards. I think, too, that what's stirring is happening at increasingly deeper layers, and this makes it more difficult to articulate.

You are going deeper and deeper into my bones, always, and the conversation we seem to be having is so marrow-borne, becoming more and more internal and increasingly intimate, it's hard to get that out, to move that from inside the marrow onto the page.

Earlier this year I began thinking about what it means to listen into the bones. On an index card, I wrote, *Listening into the bones. There's nothing that feels like it's at the surface in our conversation. The vocabulary begins in the marrow.* And on a card a couple weeks later, *What does it mean to listen into my bones? How do I do that?*

Then, just a couple months later, I broke two bones in my foot. I commented on that to Christianne in a session shortly before I came here. I told her I don't know that there's any cause and effect there, any direct correlation, but I was struck by the proximity of the questions and the mishap.

What do you make of such things?

Aside from the fact of the breaking, of the physical fractures (for which I am still wearing a boot that goes up to my knee, all around Ireland!), what do you think about those questions: *What does it mean to listen into my bones? How do I do that?*

Am I right that you are going deeper and deeper into the marrow, that the marrow is where our vocabulary begins? How do I listen into that? How do I continue to engage and enter into and sustain that conversation?

Perhaps being back here—here among these words I'm writing to you—is one of the ways I do this. That trying to articulate onto the page what's been stirring in the marrow will help.

—FRIDAY, JUNE 10, 2016—
Kenmare

Thinking some more about the room where the books begin, the room that opened up in my imagination, inspired by the space here in Ireland. A few months ago, I wrote this on an index card—a scene that arose during my quiet time that night:

> In the room where the books begin, you bring me what I need for the next pages, and leave it there for me. (Even when I don't see you.) While I sleep, you leave cookies for me, and tea, and a recording of your most recent songs. When I rise, I have what I need to get to work.

I loved that image. That you come to visit me in that place of beginning, even when I don't see you, even when I'm sleeping. You know what I need—perhaps more than I do—and you leave it as provision. I imagine that you stay with me in the resting, offering presence and solace that passes into me beyond conscious awareness. What you leave—what I find upon waking—is enough to help me create the next page, and the next.

Another scene that unfolded in the place where the books begin, jotted down in January as I prayed in the front studio: I was lingering with you at that table—that place where I had imagined you with the book that you passed your hand over, showing me wonders; the place where you had taken my hands and passed your hand over them, too, like they were pages, and showed me wonders that appeared in my hands.

Sitting with that scene as I prayed on that January night, I became particularly aware of our hands together, and I wrote: *We become transparent at the places where we connect.* The image isn't entirely clear, but I think of it as something like an X-ray—that at the points where we meet and touch, our bodies, while real, become something other or more than flesh. I don't know if it's so much that our bodies change in the meeting as that we are able to see what happens when we connect. What perhaps always happened when we connected.

That's an image I have carried close with me. And it was strange when, after I broke my foot recently, I saw my own X-rays—my own flesh made transparent.

(Ornithological interlude: I just saw a small bird on the rocks outside that I don't recall having seen before. I did a search for *Ireland bird black cap*, and, what do you know, it's a blackcap! In Gaelic, *caipín dubh.*)

As I was preparing to come to Ireland this year, I learned that the Gaelic name for this place, Neidín, means Little Nest. How lovely! And especially lovely to imagine that this is perhaps you again at work, providing for me (in my waking and my sleeping) in ways beyond what I could have imagined.

So one of the last times I wrote here, I had built a labyrinth in our home. I had written, too, some preliminary ideas about a labyrinth that was a book or a book that was a labyrinth, and I'd written about looking at the meandering book that I made at the Guild.

The idea persisted and took root. Shortly before I went up to Gainesville in February, I created some accordion book forms and took them with me, along with some art supplies I had recently acquired (embroidery thread and needles and watercolor pencils; the pencils were inspired by a piece that Mom and I had seen when we visited a gallery during one of my trips up there in January). One day, I spread my supplies out on Mom and Dad's kitchen table (my studio-away-from-studio) and began to stitch. On the first page, I stitched the word *nest* in green.

I have been loving the stitching. It's soothing and somehow seems a fitting medium for where I am right now.

Somewhere along the way, early in the process, I began calling the stitched pages the Hidden Book. It feels like a book that's just for me, for now—and for you. For us. A place of meeting. A space to explore some new techniques and to excavate this space that I, and we, are inhabiting. It feels very private and personal. (And how long has it been since I've gone into the studio simply to explore and experiment and make something for myself, without an imminent deadline?) But I've shared pages of it with a few folks, and that, too, has been its own gift and revelation.

I took some pages with me when I went to see Peg and Chuck in March. What a wondrous visit; how you inhabit our conversations. One morning, we sat on the floor of their living room, and I pulled out a couple of the boxes that had pages and papers in it. I wish I could somehow recapture the whole conversation and how precisely it was what I needed. But there are phrases and images that linger with me, snippets that I scribbled down as we talked.

Chuck talked about the theologian Terence Fretheim, how he says God is in every stitch, though it can't always be seen how God is moving back and forth through the fabric. Chuck said, *This feels like labyrinth work*, connecting the stitched pages with the labyrinth I had made in our home.

He talked about the massive forest fire that came to the edge of Holden right after they became the directors, how the fire became so big because of all the materials that had gathered on the forest floor. *It's the concentration that makes the fire possible*, he said. And as with fire, so with creative work. *Give yourself time to concentrate, to gather, to focus*, he said. *This is what makes the work possible.*

Peg said, *It's all there. Everything you need is in these two boxes. And your heart. I've never had such a fierce sense that the work you're doing right now is mission critical. This is important.*

She said, *I look at your work, and I hear you, and I know you and Gary are together. The stupid time continuum has put you in different places. But it's like everything is already in the boxes. You and Gary are working on the book together. You're the one bringing it to fruition here. The Hidden Book is a garden.*

She also said, *Someday, when the time continuum collapses, we'll figure out that we were together all along, and we had everything we needed.*

It was a pivotal conversation, and you were so much a part of it. I was especially struck by Peg's intense clarity about the Hidden Book being more important than anything I've done, and that it is, as she put it, mission critical. She said words to that effect more than once and likewise repeated, in that lovely, long conversation as we sat on the floor with the pages among us, that everything I need is in those boxes I had brought with me. Like seeds.

In another conversation, Chuck offered a fantastic image. He said, *You are diving deep, going underwater, and surfacing from time to time with a word to offer. We're in the boat, protecting you.*

Loved that.

I am so grateful for how Peg and Chuck are able to bear witness to my work and to see what's happening in the creative process. I know you know that nobody's any substitute for you, for the ways you were able to see my work with such clarity. In your physical absence, it has been a tremendous grace to have their company and their counsel at crucial points along the way. I always come away from conversations with them feeling more clear about what I'm meant to do.

It was an enormous gift to hear Peg's insistence on how important the Hidden Book is, and especially to hear this when it's such a private and personal thing for me right now—not something I'm working to put into public view anytime soon. I anticipate that some things I'm (we're?) exploring now will eventually make their way into my public work, but for now, this is between you and me, and a few trusted folks.

It might have been right after my visit with Peg and Chuck that I brought the pages of the Hidden Book to a session with Christianne. I hardly remember what we said, but it was a rich time. She commented at one point, *It's another place where he's walking into the bones.* She commented also on the front and the back of the pages—I think perhaps she was thinking especially about the process of stitching, how the needle passes back and forth between the front and back—and how you're here/not here. Can't quite capture the fullness of what she said, but it was similar to something Karen said the day I had the Tea & Solace group over and was showing them a few pages. Karen offered some beautiful words about the stitching, how it moves back and forth between front and back—that it resonated with how you move between realms.

Christianne and I have talked a fair bit about the hiddenness of the book; it might even have been with her that I first began to call it the Hidden Book. I think it was right around the time I began the Hidden Book that I came across these words by David Whyte about hiding:

HIDING
is a way of staying alive. Hiding is a way of holding ourselves until we are ready to come into the light. Hiding is one of the brilliant and virtuoso practices of almost every part of the natural world: the protective quiet of an icy northern landscape, the held bud of a future summer rose, the snowbound internal pulse of the hibernating bear. Hiding

is underestimated. We are hidden by life in our mother's womb until we grow and ready ourselves for our first appearance in the lighted world; to appear too early in that world is to find ourselves with the immediate necessity for outside intensive care.

...What is real is almost always to begin with, hidden, and does not want to be understood by the part of our mind that mistakenly thinks it knows what is happening. What is precious inside us does not care to be known by the mind in ways that diminish its presence.

...Hiding is a bid for independence, from others, from mistaken ideas we have about ourselves, from an oppressive and mistaken wish to keep us completely safe, completely ministered to, and therefore completely managed. Hiding is creative, necessary and beautifully subversive of outside interference and control. Hiding leaves life to itself, to become more of itself. Hiding is the radical independence necessary for our emergence into the light of a proper human future.

I think again of the Faddan More Psalter and the long years it spent in hiding. Centuries. More than a millennium. I marvel that it came to light. The only book ever, I think, to be found in a bog. And why did it come to light when it did? Was it any more than a mere matter of their finally coming to that layer of the bog?

What is the book I need to dig up in Ireland? The question surfaces again.

What does the book look like? What pages does it hold? What do its letters look like—what is their shape and size? Where is the book intact? Are there places it is falling apart? What holes does it hold? What can be seen through its holes? What words remain and abide? (In the Faddan More Psalter, many words remain only because the ink holds the letters together.) What if I reconfigured the letters, the words; would this result in a text that felt mixed-up, or would a deeper story be found in this way? What's happening at the edges of the pages? Where is the book buried? How will it be found? What is its name?

—Saturday, June 11, 2016—
Kenmare

Here's one of the things I'm thinking about today. On what would have been our sixth anniversary, I posted one of our wedding photos. We are standing in the field, with the lake beyond. I wrote this:

Six years ago today.

Looking at our wedding photos recently with a friend, I got chills when I realized that in this picture—the last in the series—Gary's gaze is turned directly toward the stand of palmettos where, such a brief few years later, our family would gather to bury his ashes.

I ache at the short arc of chronological time that is captured in this photo. And yet, as I have stayed with this scene, I am finding it holds a strange comfort as well. Looking at the photo with the perspective I have today—knowing now that this landscape of breathtaking joy would come to hold stunning loss—I find myself wondering what might yet be at work in this scene. What larger story is unfolding that I cannot see from here? What knowledge and vision might I one day be able to look back with—not in a way that makes the loss okay or understandable, but that enables me to see our story whole?

I find myself thinking, too, of a notion that comes to us from the lives of the Celtic saints. They were known for setting out, not knowing where they were going, yet looking for what they called "the place of our resurrection." The place of our resurrection refers both to the literal place of our burial—the spot from which we will one day be gathered into a life we can hardly now imagine—and also to the place where we come alive in this life, and learn to enter into the fullness that God desires for us here and now in this world.

Looking at this photo on this day, I am thankful for how it bears witness to both senses of "the place of our resurrection." I am thankful for how Gary and I came alive with each other, and for how, even in grief, that aliveness continues to transform my life. I am thankful for how, in the midst of our brief chronology together, we found a thin place where heaven and earth continue to meet. I am thankful for the eternity this field encompasses—an eternity I cannot yet see whole but sense in my bones.

On this day, I am thankful that (as Gary's amazing son, Emile, read from the Song of Songs at our wedding) "love is strong as death."

Stronger, I would say.

I've thought a lot about that field, both before writing the post and since. I was grateful to find a few words to begin to articulate what that photo has stirred for me. In writing about what larger story might yet be at work in the scene, it felt important to say that I wasn't looking for a story that would make the loss okay or understandable but one that would enable me to see it whole.

I continue to resist any notions about suffering that would have us believe we'll be able to see the "big picture" one day and that, once we have this big picture, we'll be able to understand the suffering. I remember being in CPE during seminary and having a lively conversation about this with my group. In a group time one day, one of them said something in that vein—I think maybe in response to some things I had shared about my work in Neonatal Intensive Care, where four babies died during my first week. I reacted strongly, expressing my doubt that anything could ever make sense of such pain.

Last night, I was weeping after coming home from dessert. I found the phrase going through my head, *I want a different story.* But of course it's not that I want a different story. We have an amazing, astoundingly wondrous story. It's that I want it to look different right now. I want November 14 not to have happened. I want the clot not to have happened. I want the aneurysm not to have happened. I want it not to have happened that the neurosurgeon walked into the room where our beloved family had been waiting for hours and hours and said, *It did not go as we anticipated.* I want it not to have happened that we had awful decisions to make as the vigil drew to a close. I want it not to have happened that we had to gather around you and let you go.

That story. That part of our story. I want that part to be different. Better.

Talking with a friend the other night who's building a house with his wife. So lovely for them, but I couldn't help but think about things you and I had talked about, how we would sometimes sit on our front porch and dream about the house we would have (and maybe build) someday.

Mostly I don't resent the beautiful plans others make. (In fact, I think I've done remarkably well with this!) They should make them. But once in a while, when I'm feeling especially alone or pathless, it's hard to take in the dreams of others. Couples, especially.

I pray that somehow we are dreaming together. That you are part of how I am dreaming. That you are with me in the dreaming. I found myself thinking again just recently about the conversation you and I had, probably less than a year before you died, where you asked, *Would you like to reimagine our life?*

Yes, I said. But I did not imagine this.

Are we doing this now? Are we finding ways to reimagine our life together even now? And I'm the one doing it in this realm, as Peg talked about.

Dreaming into the bones.

Was reading again, just last night, what David Hinton writes in *Hunger Mountain* about oracle bones—bones used for divination.

Maybe I carry my own oracle bones with me. In my flesh. And have to listen into them hard, hard, hard in order to discern the dreams that have been placed within them, the dreams that are brewing and stirring in them.

This index card, dated in March. Think I wrote this during a prayer time, when I was lingering with the image of us in the room where the books begin. I was sitting with the image that had recently come—of the place where our hands meet and touch. You were attending so closely to my hands, paying attention and working with the places where my hands met yours and were transparent. On the index card I wrote, *The words you incise on my bones. The patterns I embroider on yours.*

What are the words you incise on my bones? What patterns do I embroider on yours?

This bears more sitting with.

Earlier this spring, shortly before seeing Peg and Chuck, I had the sensation I had fallen into another room in my grieving. It felt something like what I experienced the autumn after you died—that a part of my soul had just gotten the news of your death. I had started working on the Hidden Book not long before that. (No coincidence, I'd say.) One night, when I was praying about this new layer of grief, I had the sudden realization that this was the first time I'd taken up a new medium since you had died.

That was a huge noticing.

Are you in this? I asked. Are you in the stitching and drawing and printing? Are you in these new places in my creative process, like you were so often before?

Immediately I sensed a space in my chest opening up. That same space that felt like it was being hollowed out as I was driving down to see Peg and Chuck the Epiphany after you died; that same space that feels like it's gotten larger and larger. It was remarkable to experience it, to notice such an immediate response in my body as I sensed that space opening.

I wanted to take it as a *yes* that you are in this: every stitch, every line. That the Hidden Book is a place of meeting, a place where you are present, a place of revelation and knowing.

On the index card where I wrote about that realization and that sensation of opening, I had written this at the top: *Walking (falling) into a new room of grief. Secret room.* Thinking, of course, about Phil Cousineau's words in *The Art of Pilgrimage*, where he writes about the secret rooms that wait for us when we are on pilgrimage. In this time when I am feeling like such a stranger in my own life and wondering how it might feel instead to become a pilgrim in this strange landscape and strange time, I have thought about secret rooms. Aware that even in landing—hard—in what I could only describe as a new room in grief, it had something of that sense of being a secret room.

It occurred to me that even as exposed as I feel in my grief—increasingly exposed as new places open up within it—that exposure also means there are more places in me where I can meet you. I think maybe it was Christianne who, when I was talking about this one day, commented that this means there's more of me that you can access. It resonates, too, with something Peg said in the conversation I shared about yesterday. I had told her and Chuck about falling into this new layer of grief and the sensation that another corner of my soul had just gotten the news you had died. Peg said, *I think it's really courageous to let yourself know the news that Gary is dead. That's an incredible way to let Gary enter. That's a path.*

But of course not to go seeking out new layers of grief just for the purpose of providing greater access. I quite trust the new layers will appear all on their own, in their own time.

I don't know that falling into that new room was triggered by anything in particular. Simply by time, perhaps. Simply because that part of my soul was ready to open. To receive the terrible news.

It occurs to me now to wonder: Is this secret room—the new room of grief I fell into—connected in any way with the room where the books begin?

Hm. That's something to sit with. Are they the same? Do they overlap? As I fall into new rooms of grief, do they give me more access to the place where the books begin—that place where I encounter you?

—Monday, June 13, 2016—
Kenmare

More labyrinth thoughts.

One of the things I loved about creating the triple spiral

labyrinth in our home is that it was inspired by the one at the Guild. I love the design of that labyrinth and especially love that it's one I walked with you.

On an index card in March, I wrote these words: *ladder and labyrinth*. Words that surfaced in my prayer time. It reminds me of the dream I had, I think in the early months after you died, where we were learning how to balance or somehow dance on a ladder and how resonant the image of the ladder was with the work we had done with the story of Jacob. How I still love the ladder of his story, the ladder that emerges in his dreaming, the ladder that becomes a thin place, the ladder that links heaven and earth and bears witness to the connection between the realms.

The ways a labyrinth does this. How it is something like a ladder in the horizontal, a curving ladder that becomes a path, one that in its own way can become a thin place and a place of meeting between worlds.

How I am still learning to walk the labyrinth. How I am still learning to walk the labyrinth with you, to find my footing on this ladder between heaven and earth.

Several nights later in my prayer time, a scene unfolded of being with you in the room where the books begin. The room sometimes opens onto a courtyard (sometimes it opens onto other things; it's a wonderfully fluid room). On that night, there was a labyrinth in the courtyard—a lovely old stone labyrinth. You and I were sitting beside it. On an index card I wrote, *Sparrows on the labyrinth tonight. We feed them. Everything here is Eucharist.*

Loved that notion, that knowing that somehow, everything that appears in that room, everything that happens in that space that has opened up in my imagination—that it is all part of Eucharist. That it is sacrament. This doesn't help it hurt any less, doesn't make me grieve any less. But it seems that part of what a sacrament does is to offer a space to our brokenness, to make room within our rending, and to welcome and hold and tend the broken pieces, trusting there is sustenance within and among the fragments.

You don't need a labyrinth. You are *a labyrinth.* Maru said this to me in a conversation in February. She also said, *I heard the scripture, "She is flesh of my flesh and bone of my bones."*

Flesh of my flesh. I so appreciated Maru reminding me of this verse. Having just written about Eucharist, it strikes me that this passage from Genesis so resonates with what Jesus says and does at the Last Supper. *This is my body. This is my blood.* That when we share in this, we share in his flesh, his life.

So, having shared with such intimacy in your life, being flesh of your flesh and bone of your bones (*the bones again; how do I listen into those bones?*), what do I do now that your flesh is gone from this world? In the place where you abide, in the place where you are now, do you have flesh and bone and blood, or perhaps some kind of embodiment I can hardly imagine or fathom from here? If so, do I still somehow share in that now, as one who was one with you, flesh and bone, in this life, in this world? What does it mean to participate in that, when I live, as Maru talked about in February, with the fading nature of embodiment in this world—this world where your body no longer is? (Not visibly, at any rate.) What does it mean that we are both part of the body of Christ, that we each participate in this body, in his body? What does this mean for us in relationship?

Another index card I brought to Ireland with me. This one, dated January, says: *The love is the same both sides of the veil.*

Those words most likely surfaced in prayer. I remember their arriving as a comfort, a solace. That amid all my questions—and the questions are many, and deep, and keen—this seems to be something to hang on to: That no matter where you are, no matter what the shape of your life is now, the love we shared before your death is congruent with the love we share now. That while you are likely experiencing this love differently now, perhaps there is something about it that is familiar to you. That it may be changing in its expression but has not altered at its core. That the love that grew and deepened and abided between us throughout your time here is of the same stuff that continues to live between us now, is part of the same tissue that drew us together. That the rending changes the tissue but does not destroy it or fundamentally alter it.

Bone of my bones, flesh of my flesh. This reminds me of something

Maru shared in a session last December. I don't recall exactly what led up to it, but she said, *It's the difference between having a relationship and being one with someone.*

I've thought about those words a lot. They get at what's both so wonderful and so challenging about being in conversation with you now. When a conversation happens in the bones, in the marrow—when it happens within the space of oneness—it's wonderfully personal and intimate and close, and that's beautiful. But it can be confusing and lonely; it can be overwhelming to deal with how different it is to have that conversation instead of a face-to-face conversation where expressions can be read and questions asked and meanings clarified. Where we can see and be seen by one another. This way—talking to each other through the marrow, the heart, the blood—can stir doubts and loneliness. And it gets so hideously painful sometimes to be having the conversation without being able to see your face, to hold on to you, to be gathered in the shelter of your arms.

Stood and took a stretch break just now. Looked out these beautiful glass walls and thought, *Ireland has a lot of slow rain.* This made me smile—the thought that you brought me to this place that has slow rain, in which time moves differently.

Also from the index card from my conversation with Maru last December: *Tomb—it's time to walk and trust that the light and the presence go with you. Love—not just out there but in here. The love is there—it's not fabricated. The more relaxed and trusting you are, the more you live into that love, and it comes and greets you.*

Beautiful image—that the love comes and greets me. And her assurance that the love is there—that it's not fabricated, not made up. That if I can lean into it, relax into it, trust it, I will live into it. That it will meet me every time.

Yes.

Deep breath.

Thinking more about how the conversation between us happens.

At some point after I began working on the Hidden Book, I was beautifully struck by how the notion of creating this book began as I was walking the labyrinth I had created in our home—walking and thinking, *It would be really cool to create a book that's a labyrinth or a labyrinth that's a book.* And the idea of creating the labyrinth in our home began in one of my prayer times, when an image came of you and me walking a labyrinth together, one in which we meet not only across space but across time as well. (Or deeply within time, or however that works.)

Working on the Hidden Book, tracing the path of how it came to be, I thought, *This is how the conversation happens.* Part of how it happens, at least. The way that ideas or images come, take root, draw me down the path, form connections, bring solace, open me more deeply to you. It came as a beautiful realization, giving some language to how it is, or how it might be, that the conversation continues to unfold between us.

Help me continue to pay attention to what comes to the surface. Help me allow it to come to the surface in the first place. To notice. To carry. To respond. To let it speak.

—TUESDAY, JUNE 14, 2016—
Kenmare

I was all ready to head to my writing space around noontime, but then my stomach said, *Hey, how about lunch first?* So I made a detour to Jam, where I had a tasty sandwich and wrote and ate and ate and wrote.

One of the blessings I worked on at lunch—the idea for which just arrived at lunch—is one whose working title is "Blessing for Getting the News." Working on it took me back to the moment when your neurosurgeon came into the waiting room at 4 a.m. and told us the terrible news. I remember very little beyond his first sentence, only a noise in my brain that overtook everything else.

A lovely bit showed up at what might be the end of the blessing. The rough version of that bit is:

May the humming
give way to song
even if it will
be long and long
before you can
hear it,
can hear the
love
that latched onto you
in the rending
and has never
let you go.

That came as a surprise and a gift to me—the idea that even in the disaster that happened in surgery, even in your dying and your physical leaving, your love latched onto me in a new way and has not let me go. Ever.

I pray to feel this, to *know* this in my brain and my bones. I think my bones know it. My brain often has a more difficult time. I would like to think that, ultimately, my brain is not the boss of me. (Right.) That where my brain has a hard time believing that you abide, that you love me still, that I will know you face to face again someday, my heart will move in, working on the disbelief, being medicine and balm to it.

In another part of a conversation earlier this year, in which we were talking (again) about the part of me that has a hard time believing you abide, Maru said, *I'm wondering if you can connect with the part of you that doesn't need proof.* She wondered how it might be for me to let the doubting voice be one of the voices in the circle but not the only voice.

I like that notion—that it's not necessarily a choice between doubt and belief, as it typically seems, but that doubt and belief are among the voices in my circle right now. Each has something to say. It's important to listen, but I don't have to give every voice equal weight, equal say. Still, it's hard not to.

She mentioned a question that appears in the Grail legends: *Whom does the Grail serve?* Don't remember precisely the point she made about that, but I think perhaps it had to do with asking questions of the voices, or letting the voices ask the questions they need to ask, or asking each voice whom or what it serves. Actually, I like that—asking the voices that come up, *Whom do you serve?*

Whom or what does the doubting voice serve? The believing voice? The lonely voice? The scared voice? The fierce voice?

Will have to sit with those.

On the index card from that conversation, I also wrote: *Narnia—faith.* I think this was Maru talking about how it's those who have faith who are able to find their way to Narnia. Faith, perhaps, and I think the ability to be surprised and not question everything they see when they find themselves in a strange place. Thinking of Lucy, the first time she wanders into Narnia. She doesn't straight away think she's gone crazy. She's able to see and receive it. Though she will need to develop some healthy suspicion and discernment and cunning. Can't take every faun at face value.

I sometimes wonder if, amidst all the ways I seek to pay attention to my grieving, to listen into it, I am truly open to the thin place between us, to your presence. Sometimes that wondering takes a dark turn: *Am I listening well? Am I listening correctly?* I try to let those questions have their say but not to linger with them and with the doubts they harbor.

But I do want to know what it means to listen well, to be open to how you might show up, to discern how you are moving in my bones, my blood, my heart. To know and live into the love that is present on both sides of the veil. To be engaged in the ongoing conversation with you, even as I continue to listen my way into my life that is unfolding on this side of the veil. I continue to be persuaded that listening for you is part of how I'm meant to listen my way into my unfolding life.

What does it mean to listen?

Just today I found myself thinking of a day some time ago when the words surfaced: *You must be very still.* The words came with a sense that in the stillness I would find you, that the stillness would be a place of meeting. The stillness seems to come with a craving for space, for being able to have room to breathe and not feel pressed by my schedule. I think that's part of what drove my decision to make some choices for rest this past year, especially with not doing the online retreats. That the rest, the stillness, and the space have been necessary for the listening—not only for you, but for the life I am making.

Just noticed a scene I would love to have a snapshot of but wouldn't be able to capture well because of the distance, and also because he moved quickly off: the image of one of the hooded crows that I've so enjoyed here, sitting on an arched iron gate on one of the balconies across from my writing space, gray clouds gathered in the background. All very moody and Gothic. I love these crows.

Finally, for now: this note from a conversation with Maru in February: *David—psalm—Why are you cast down, O my soul?* From Psalm 43. Reminds me of what I was feeling one morning last week, when I was weeping before I even got out of bed. I thought, *How can I be sad in Ireland? It seems ungrateful.*

But real.

But the psalmist ends that psalm with this: *Hope in God; for I shall again praise him, my help and my God.*

I shall again praise him. Haven't checked how the tense works in the Hebrew, but in the English translation, it has the sense of, *I'm finding it too difficult to praise God right now, but I will praise*

God again one day. I am cast down and disquieted now, but hope is stubborn, and I will give praise again one day.

Till then—and probably even then—I'll let the anger have its say, and the sorrow; I'll let the rage speak its mind; I'll give despair a voice, and doubt, and keep an eye open for what comes even in the dissonance.

—Friday, July 15, 2016—

Sad. Sad. Sad. I was doing some work in our studio just now—watercolor pencil on muslin, preliminary work for some new pages in the Hidden Book—and, as I worked, a memory stirred of being in Savannah with you. How long ago now? One of the only times we took something of a vacation together.

Those days of ambling through the town with you, exploring the squares, browsing through a bookstore, stopping afterward at that lovely café where you began reading the book I had bought for you and I began reading the book you had bought for me. The utter contentment and pleasure of being with you, of walking through this world together. You would propose to me there—two years later? Three?

Ireland helped. Something feels loosened a bit around my heart. I came home with a stack of blessings in progress. Somewhere in that first week, when I was still struggling with where to turn my writing attention, I decided to approach the blessing-writing as an excavation process, not worrying about coming home with polished pieces but focusing on getting as much raw material as possible down on paper. It was an excellent move; I needed to take that pressure off myself to come home with finished work.

I'm intrigued by what emerged in the blessings as I worked in Ireland, writing from the place I am now. Sensing you are still at work in the blessings. I ran out of paper and began to write new blessings on the backs of existing blessings I had in the binder. Something heartening and lovely about seeing the layering of blessings—blessings I wrote while you were still alive, blessings I wrote in the initial year or two after your death, and blessings I am writing now. Sensing you are present in all the layers of the blessings.

It was an excellent move also to let myself write here in these pages, especially in that first week when I wasn't feeling much energy for writing blessings. I needed this space. And letting myself be here, I think, helped make some room for the blessings finally to begin to come as my time in Kenmare unfolded. I love how, in addition to making their way to my table in my writing space, they also began to turn up in other places, particularly at mealtimes. Scribbling down bits and pieces of blessings as I ate.

Some significant shifting has taken place in the wake of coming home from Ireland. Hard to find words for it.

PART SEVEN
Little Nest

NESTED

Say I was nested.
Say your wing over me.

Say gathered
and sheltered.

Say warmed
and safe.

All night.
All night.

—Tuesday, May 23, 2017—
*Kenmare** *

The folks upstairs woke me with their footfalls at 5:45 this morning. It didn't last long, but there was no going back to sleep at that point, despite trying for a bit. It's just after six now. I am cranky about being awake, particularly with not being over the jet lag yet, but it is beautiful as I look out this window, my feet propped on the sill. Everything is green, with a mist mantling it all. The birds have begun their concert for the day. Yesterday I spied the hooded crows I so came to love last year. Their beautiful black and dusky gray, the gray tracing more of a cloak than a hood.

Thinking about sleep, I wonder again, do you sleep where you are? I hope so. I want to curl up with you and rest for a long, long time.

I have this imagining—it began some time ago—that you sleep when I sleep and wake when I wake. That it's one of your ways of staying close, of being with me, of making sure there is no moment of the day when I am completely alone.

Do you dream? I first asked you this some time ago and still wonder.

When I came to Ireland two years ago with Karen and the gang, I dreamed of you on our first night here in Kenmare. You stood before me, arms outstretched, your face radiant with joy and compassion. With no words, you gathered me in. That was all I remembered when I woke that morning—the morning of June 2, exactly a year and a half since you had died. It was enough of the dream, remembering you enfolding me. It felt like a welcome to Ireland, a welcome to Kenmare, a welcome to this place that would become so dear to me and full of solace.

Last night, after walking back from dinner, Karen and I spent time downstairs, listening to the lovely pianist. We sat in the alcove, tucked amongst the windows that look onto Kenmare Bay. At one point I looked out at the darkening landscape, commented to

Except for the final two entries, this section was written in Kenmare, Ireland.

Karen on the mist that draped itself across the hills. *How many thin places out there?* I said. *Maybe it's all a thin place here.*

Without romanticizing this place. Without minimizing the pain Ireland has known. Without glossing over the normal (and beyond normal) difficulties anyone lives with in any place.

But there is something particular in this place. Talking a couple evenings ago with John, who runs the bar at the Park, telling him of the solace I have found here. *It seems like Ireland has this vast capacity for holding sorrow and for knowing how to transform it,* I said to him. And his vigorous nod, his understanding of the pain of this place and of the generations who have learned to turn this pain into art, into story, into song.

I think of Yeats, who wrote about the dead being nearer here. I came across the quote in a beautiful novel I picked up here last year—*History of the Rain* by Niall Williams. *In Ireland,* Yeats wrote, *this world and the world we go to after death are not far apart.* Perhaps this is a romantic notion as well, an idealization, but when I first read it, it rang true. There is something about the lay of this land that disposes it toward thin places, that cannot help but gather those places into its landscape; something here that inspires the dead to linger, not in a way that hinders them from entering into whatever happens next but that enables them never to be very far from here, or at least always to return and to find some kind of home here.

I can imagine this is true also for those who never knew Ireland in this life. Like you. With its capacity for holding both sorrow and joy, with its ability to find and ring the deep chords between them, and with its memory that is impossibly long and immeasurably deep—I can imagine this land has a way of drawing the dead to it. Or at least that for those of us who live or visit here, the landscape and the being of this country help make it possible for us to perceive, to imagine, to open to what is sometimes more difficult to perceive elsewhere.

Is it possible that in this place, I might hold more loosely all those questions about whether you abide, whether you exist in a form I will be able to know and touch one day when my own life here is finished? Perhaps I need to add this to the list of questions stirring for me in Ireland this time.

What does it mean for you that Gary might abide? Karen asked as we talked here one day.

That there is an ongoingness to you. That you have not simply disappeared or been absorbed into some cosmic ooze. That something of the Gary I knew continues. That I will come face to face with this—with you—someday.

I talked with Karen of how the abiding is not merely a some-day thing. If you abide, I think you abide even now. That you have consciousness. That you have presence. That the persistence that so marked you in this life (I think of the tae kwon do award for perse-verance that is still in your studio) is part of you still. That wherever you are, you are figuring out how to be present to me in the ways you can—the ways that help me imagine and make a new life here, even as you imagine and make a new life where you are, which is perhaps not as elsewhere as it seems.

I am not feeling terribly resilient these days—I was talking with Karen about this just a day or two ago—but I do think you and I have this persistence, this lovely stubbornness, that enables us to find whatever connections are possible between us at this point in our path—without hindering our path, without keeping either of us stuck in our grief.

It's coming up on seven o'clock, and I think I'll try slipping back into bed, seeing if sleep comes again.

From this window, from this green and shrouded and compel-ling landscape where perhaps you linger near, I bless you and I love you, Sweetheart. Let's get some rest now.

I'm just in from a lovely walk, which helped my soul do some catching up with the rest of me. Walked through town and then on the paths in Reenagross Park. Spent time down by the river, looking at stones. Brought a few back to the room, possibly to do some stitching and wrapping with them.

I've done lots of stitching since the spring of last year. I'm not sure yet where it's leading me, but it still feels resonant, a fitting medium for me right now. I'm continuing to let myself explore, trying to work on it without agenda or deadlines or pressure to figure it out. It feels like I'm working to find a vocabulary with the stitching—a style, a way of working.

One of the things I began experimenting with in the past couple of months has been stitching small pieces of muslin (usually pieces I'd painted with watercolor last year) and wrapping them around smooth stones—some of the stones I used for the labyrinth I built in our home last year. I've stitched some wrappings with words, then turned the text to the inside, next to the stone. I love the look of the reverse of the writing; it feels like a secret message, part of the Hidden Book. Each wrapped stone feels like a little story, a talisman, something mysterious I don't quite understand but is solid inside.

It has not escaped me that there's something shroud-ish about them, and perhaps about much of the work I've been doing with the muslin and also with linen. That awareness—that there is something of a shroud in these pieces—draws me back to your last day and how, sometime after your death, I began to wish I could have remained present longer than I did, could have done a different or better job of attending your body, what was left of the earthly you, in those moments after you died. I found your appearance so disturbing, so wrenching and incomprehensible—how rapidly your appearance changed. One of the nurses had warned me. *Desaturation will happen quickly*, she told me. *Desaturation*. What a strange word, applied to you, to your body, so beautiful and beloved.

But I think I will save thinking on that, writing about that, for another day.

I am sitting by the window. The sky has darkened. I can just see the outline of the ridge of trees against the sky and a few lights across the way, reflecting in the water. Crows cry, as they have done all day. A nearly constant chorus. Normally my sound-sensitive self would find such a thing unbearable, and I may well do before long, but for now there is something about their call that is—not comforting, exactly, but there is something of solace in it. Maybe it's a vestige of the girl who wanted to become an ornithologist when she grew up—that her imagination was touched and opened by birds, who knew how to inhabit both sky and earth.

O let me be that bird of two worlds / In the blinding blue, you would sing. *To dive into the mirror of the lake / As I was meant to do.*

The radio plays quietly in a corner of the room. The crow cries give way to the opening song of the station's nighttime program. I listen as I watch the dark spread itself across the green hills. *Alleluia*, a gorgeous chorus of voices is singing. *Alleluia, alleluia.*

Alleluia for you, Sweetheart.

Alleluia, Sparrow.

I love you this night and always.

—FRIDAY, JUNE 2, 2017—

I am thinking about the gaps—the gaps in our story that were caused by your death; the gaps (huge, gigantic, aching gaps) in my life as I live without having you here, in the flesh; the gaps in my own telling of the story—my story, our story—in these pages. I don't want to dwell overmuch on what I haven't been able to do in these crushing years and what I haven't been able or willing to write in these pages, this space.

Thinking of how often, when it came to writing here, I have been saddened into silence. Grieved into silence. Wearied into silence. Depressed into silence.

But thinking also of how my silence here has sometimes been because so much was stirring—connections being made, illumination suddenly showing forth—and I could hardly begin to capture it here, on the page. I hope something of this made its way into my artwork, especially over the past year—the stitching, stitching, stitching I have done, looking for the threads and trying to make a way.

Sitting down at my (our?) writing table when I arrived a few minutes ago, gathering myself as I entered this space that has gathered me in, I found myself thinking of John O'Donohue, where he writes about there being a place where our unlived lives gather. I have found this enormously comforting as I think about pathways that closed themselves to me, to us, as not meant for this life. Is there a place where we get to live some of those lives?

I wonder if—I hope—there is also a place where my unwritten pages gather. The pages I was too sad or tired to write or where I was inexplicably visited with wonders that seemed too rich to try to capture in words. Is there a place where those pages have gathered themselves, or where you have gathered them? Is there a place where you have been able to write some of that for me, or a place you are keeping until I arrive and can write those pages down?

The room where the books begin, perhaps.

In thinking about the gaps in these pages, I have sometimes thought about the ancient Irish book-shrines, the exquisite containers worked in metal that held a book, usually a manuscript of the gospels. A book-shrine would have been kept on an altar. There are some that, once the book was enclosed, were never intended to be opened again. Viewing the book was not the point. It was enough to know that it was there, sacred and holy. That the power of the pages did not lie in being seen. That the story they contained did not depend on being read. That the story imbued the space, the people, with its presence. Took flesh in them.

It seems counterintuitive that something of such beauty should be hidden away. Greedy, somehow. And yet there is something powerful about it, something comforting. That looking, seeing, understanding is not always the purpose. That our story, the sacred text of our lives, gathers itself nonetheless—the terrible pages, the beautiful pages, the pages marked by pain and loss, the pages limned with wonder and unexpected joy—and there is something of this that is necessarily secret and hidden away, sometimes even from ourselves.

But I wonder if there are pages you can perceive—pages of your life, of mine—that were unreadable and unknowable in this life. If you have been able to get a glimpse into the pages that gathered themselves—those unlived or unwritten pages. I wonder what you are writing now in the place where you are and whether you have mediums and dimensions at hand for creating things I can scarcely imagine from here. And I wonder what you see of my life. I think of your remarkable gift for knowing me—*I see you,* you told me—and how adept you were at seeing what was stirring in my life and in my work, sometimes before it made itself known to me.

You were part of how my life made itself known to me.

And now, in the physical absence of you, so much of that knowing happens in secrecy, in silence. In the gaps. There are ways, in these past months, I have become intentional about moving with the silence and hiddenness. I think again of David Whyte and what he says about hiddenness. I have chosen to be less visible, less exposed—to secret myself away in the studio, for example, where I am exploring without agenda or deadlines, needing to see what happens there when I allow that room, that space, that time. To let what happens there be secret for now. Even, sometimes, from myself, as I stitch and paint without knowing just where it is leading me.

Praying there is something holy in that hiddenness. A shrine. Something that holds a story whose power, beauty, and grace are not lessened by not being visible.

Here's what O'Donohue writes about unlived lives in *To Bless the Space Between Us*:

> What happened to the lives you once had as options but did not choose? Where do they dwell? Perhaps your unlived lives run parallel to your current life and in some subtle way continue to influence the choices you make. All this might be happening beside you and in you, yet unknown to you. Maybe these unlived yet still unfolding lives are the

sustenance from which your chosen life draws. Maybe this is one of the secrets of death: that you die only when your invisible, unchosen lives have also fulfilled themselves, so that you bring into the eternal world not only your one known life but also the unknown, unchosen lives as well. Maybe your visible life is but the outer edge of a whole enterprise of creativity and realization in which you are unknowingly involved. This unseen ground of your unfolding in the world is a place that needs blessing and holds the key to the invisible. Blessing strengthens the network of presence you carry through the world.

Maybe that's another way of seeing the gaps. That they're not simply made of absence, of what is missing or torn away from our visible and known life. Perhaps they are an opening into *a whole enterprise of creativity and realization.* An entryway into that place of creativity and unfolding, where, I hope, you dwell in a fullness and completeness and ongoingness that we had only glimpses of here. (But what glimpses!)

I'm struck by what O'Donohue writes about this unseen ground of unfolding being a place that needs blessing and that it holds the key to the invisible. (*Key.* I flash back to that Advent conversation with Karen, Kathy, and Barbara, just weeks after you died—how I talked about wanting to find keys that would help me not feel so locked into this "grief process.")

How would it be to bless this place, these gaps? In some ways I feel like that's what so much of my life and my work and my writing have been about these past few years. Blessing, blessing, blessing. Blessing the painful places. Blessing the broken places. Blessing the places of aching and rending. Blessing the places of anger and of sorrow that feels nearly unspeakable. But to speak it. How this in itself is an act of blessing. To speak the sorrow. To speak into the sorrow. To let the sorrow itself speak, to let it have its say even when I don't want to hear anymore, can hardly bear to hear what it has to say, pouring from the inside of my bones, pounding in my beating heart.

And in the pouring, somehow a blessing. And in the pounding of my heart, somehow a blessing. And in the gaps, somehow a blessing that gathers itself even now, that has been gathering itself for ages, that will never stop.

A blessing whose words perhaps you know, and whose cadence you can sense and sing.

Please help me to hear it and to bring some measure of it forth in this world.

I think of your song "May We Find You," inspired by the discovery of the Faddan More Psalter. The story you sometimes told when you sang it, how you closed the story with the image of the long-ago monk who perhaps had lost or buried the psalter and the man who, a thousand years later, found it in the bog: the image of the two of them holding it together at the corners, the span of a millennium as nothing in the mind of God.

Is this perhaps how it works here too? That the blessings I am finding my way to, the books I am laboring to bring forth—you already hold the other edge of them, with me and for me?

I have thought of such a thing in my stitching, how just recently the image came of you holding the other end of the cloth.

I have found my way to Poffs for lunch, just off Henry Street. Tried it with Karen for the first time a few days ago. A very yummy lunch. It is a gorgeous, sunny day, rumored to be the last one for a while. After a couple hours in my writing spot, I slipped outside, ready to move from seeing the sunshine to being out in it. Had planned to find a lunch table outside. But once outside, I found it a good bit nippier than I had anticipated. But Poffs is a good in-between. I'm at a table by the doors, which are wide open. There is a beautiful tulip in a small vase on the table, radiating its own perfection.

It makes me think of the whirring I heard through the window as I was trying to convince myself to get out of bed this morning. When I finally rose and looked outside, I saw a fellow with a weed whacker, doing murder to the beautiful little flowers that grow wild on the lawn. It reminded me of when you would mow our lawn, how before you began mowing, you would pick some of the tiny flowers that grew wild in our yard, bring them into our house, put them in a little vase, and give them to me. Loved, loved, loved that. Thank you for that practice, that ritual of kindness and grace.

Today is June 2. Three and a half years since you died. I hardly know where to begin with that. Perhaps with offering thanks, with speaking gratitude and gladness for the fact of being here in Ireland on June 2 this year, and June 2 last year, and June 2 the year before. Gladness for the generous friend who has gifted me with time here the past two years. Gladness for the hospitality of people I have crossed paths with in this kind town. Gladness for a place in Ireland that has made a place in my heart, a place I am coming to know. Gladness for the nesting that has been provided here, even before I knew the Gaelic name for Kenmare is Neidín, Little Nest. Gladness for the wonder of being here. Gladness for the gladness that persists through the enduring sorrow, including the sorrow that we never traveled to Ireland together. But gladness in the wondering if you are present in this now, and perhaps that you, who I have so often asked to make a nesting for me, found this way to offer a nest and sanctuary and shelter.

These past few days, as this three-and-a-half-year marker has drawn near, I have been thinking about the woman from Revelation 12, the woman John sees in his vision of the end. She is clothed with the sun, John tells us, with the moon beneath her feet and a crown of twelve stars about her head. A celestial woman. She is in labor, John writes; *travailing in birth*, the King James Version tells it, *and pained to be delivered* (v. 3). The dragon waits at her feet, poised to devour the son she is bringing forth.

You know this story. You sang about this in your song "O There Is a Shelter." How help is given, how her child is taken up to heaven before the dragon can destroy, how the woman flees to a place of safety that has been prepared for her by God:

Time and times and half a time
Out of the reach of this struggling world
Time and times and half a time
You have prepared a place

You know this story: how the dragon makes war upon the earth and goes after the woman once again:

Take me away from this trouble
That hunts me like a hungry beast
I cannot bear it
I cannot bear it
The way that thing
Is looking at me

And then, and then, how the woman is given the two wings of the great eagle and flies to the wilderness, to the place where she can stay for a time and times and half a time.

Three and a half years. Revelation counts it out earlier in the chapter: one thousand two hundred and seventy-eight days.

And here at my own three and a half years, here at my time and times and half a time, I am thinking about wilderness and shelter, about dragons and danger and devastation, about what has been taken away and what given.

When I finished *The Cure for Sorrow* last fall, Christianne gave me a wondrous gift: a beautifully framed reproduction of two images from one of the marvelous illuminated Apocalypses created in England in the thirteenth century. In the top scene, an illumination of the woman receiving wings. In the scene below, the woman fleeing to the wilderness. It is a gorgeous gift.

I love that in the second scene, the artist has depicted the woman with a book. It's probably a gospel book. As with many medieval images of Mary, who is often depicted with a book, it likely signified the presence of Christ the Word. But I am taken by the notion that, at the ending of the world she had known, the woman simply needed a book she could take with her into the wilderness.

For a time and times and half a time.

Maybe it's not a gospel book. Maybe it's the text of her life—the book where the unknown, unwritten pages of her story have gathered themselves. In the wilderness, in the shelter, she can come to read them. To know them. To write them.

Wearing her wings:

O there is a shelter
O there is a shelter
O there is a safe and sheltered place
O there is a shelter
O there is a shelter
Give me wings to fly into your grace

And I think of the shelter that has been provided these past three and a half years. The wondrous refuge given by my family, who have each found their own way to be amazing. I want to list them, to name those ways, but it feels like one of those times when it seems overwhelming to try to give words enough to how Scott and Lacinda have looked after me, how Sally and Craig have provided hospitality and shelter in Toronto, how Mom and Dad continue to be such a place of refuge.

And the sanctuary provided for me in Kenmare, this little nest, this place where I have found light and space and time to breathe, to write some of the pages of my unwritten book, to take something of that book back home with me.

The past three and a half years have not been unremitting shelter and sanctuary. Or have not always felt that way. Keenly aware of the persistence of grief, of sorrow, of pain. The sense of exposure and danger that grief is so good at. The celestial woman's shelter was in the wilderness, after all. And wilderness has a way of making itself known, of pressing into even the strongest sanctuaries. But to look back and know how, encompassing the grief I have traveled with so intensely, there has been a circle of—well, let's say a circle of grace, a shelter fashioned by so many hands, a refuge that is vaster even than the grief.

But here's a question: What does the woman do at the end of three and a half years? After a time and times and half a time have passed, what time comes next? John is silent on this point. It's not part of his vision, or if it is, he's not telling.

And for me, on this day that marks a time and times and half a time since your dying and since landing hard in this wilderness your death propelled me toward—what comes next? Some things seem clear. Working on these pages, which seem to be gathering themselves into a book called *Sparrow*. More time in the studio. What else? What next?

I think of the wilderness to which the winged woman flew. How the wilderness is, again and again, a threshold place, a between-place. A *betwixt* place. (Peg used that word when I last saw her and Chuck.) How it is permeable, its borders indefinite, its boundaries not always sure. How it is inhabited by wonders and by strange beasts. Christ in the desert, his own wilderness days. *And he was with the wild beasts*, Mark's Gospel tells us. And tells us this too: *And the angels waited on him* (v. 13).

And for a time and times and half a time, there have been wild beasts wandering through this wilderness I am in, with their grace both fierce and tender. There have been wings as well, angels come to offer their grace that is nearly unbearable. How tender and fierce it, too, is.

I wonder if this is a threshold I will always live on in some way. I suspect yes. I think of Jane Hirshfield and her words about the threshold life—how this is a place some are called to live, to make a home. The questions I have lived with on this threshold: *Is this a place where I am being called to rest or to stretch myself in a new direction? How long am I meant to be in this place of hiddenness, and when will it be time to move beyond this place, to be less enclosed and hidden?*

Sitting here on this bright day in Ireland—this place of thresholds and thin places—I wonder if the questions have not so much to do with how and when I will move across this threshold but with how I will continue to make a home—a home that's expansive enough to allow for movement and unhiding and crossing, a home in which I'll know what time it is, what time it's for. A threshold

that finds a home in me. A threshold I will keep making and making again.

A threshold I make with you, I hope. I pray.

Heaven is full of the membranes of lost manuscripts.

Came across this line today while reading *The Vintner's Luck*, a
curious novel by Elizabeth Knox that I found at one of the stalls at
the Wednesday Market.

This unceasing curiosity about what has been lost and whether
what has been lost remains lost forever.

Thinking of a poem that turned up for me earlier this year. The
poet, Rebecca Lindenberg, wrote it after the death of her husband,
also a poet:

In the Museum of Lost Objects

> *What thou lov'st well shall not be reft from thee;*
> *What thou lov'st well is thy true heritage.*
> Ezra Pound

You'll find labels describing what is gone:
an empress's bones, a stolen painting

of a man in a feathered helmet
holding a flag-draped spear.

A vellum gospel, hidden somewhere long ago
forgotten, would have sat on that pedestal;

this glass cabinet could have kept the first
salts carried back from the Levant.

To help us comprehend the magnitude
of absence, huge rooms

lie empty of their wonders—the Colossus,
Babylon's Hanging Gardens and

in this gallery, empty shelves enough to hold
all the scrolls of Alexandria.

My love, I've petitioned the curator
who has acquired an empty chest

representing all the poems you will
now never write. It will be kept with others

in the poet's gallery. Next door,
a vacant room echoes with the spill

of jewels buried by a pirate who died
before disclosing their whereabouts.

I hope you don't mind, but I have kept
a few of your pieces

for my private collection. I think
you know the ones I mean.

Hard to write what I felt as I read this poem. (The words to describe it are lost.) I think of the lostness of what was and has vanished; the lostness of what never came to be. Right now the latter feels like the more keen loss, if a comparison can even be made.

Is there something here that can become unlost or perhaps is not lost in the ways I thought?

The girl who was fascinated by extinct birds, by endangered birds. I spoke of this with Christianne one day—how I read about them, wrote about them, drew pictures of them, subjected my family to presentations about them. It was my first experience of articulating absence—questioning it, creating with it, trying to wrap my head around how something can become *gone*.

I need that language now, I wrote after that conversation with Christianne. A vocabulary to trace the goneness, the absence; a language that will make the absence more than that, more than a vanishing. The language I have been working on finding here, in these pages—in the lines and in the gaps between them. There are days it seems like nothing so much as a sad inversion: these lines are here because you are not.

A question tickling my brain that I cannot quite articulate, a wondering. Thinking of the Museum of Lost Objects and of that line about heaven being full of the membranes of lost manuscripts. Wondering whether there is something you are able to manifest in this world from where you are. If something exists here because you are there. That the force of your soul, your presence, your creativity is that strong. That whatever it is, it is more than a ghostly lingering, an afterimage of something that was once here and whose substance is now gone. Not like an offset left in a book by the page opposite or by something slipped inside it and forgotten. New page. Fresh ink.

Looking up the definition of *offset*, I find this: *cessation*, with the example *rapid regular beating of the heart . . . characterized by sudden onset and sudden* offset.

I want to believe that the offset—of your heart, of your life— was not the last thing, was not the final word. That what remains is other than an echo, other than shadow, other than phantom pain. That there is more here than a gap, a rend, a hole around which I keep tracing useless circles.

But I think of Tess in "After the Chinese"—*I've worn a little path, an egg-shaped circle / around your grave keeping warm / while I talk to you*, she writes. And, soon after, *No one / is as stubborn as me.* Maybe I am not just spinning my wheels, my brain, my heart. Or if I am, perhaps there is something of the Sufi in it, the dervish given to whirling, whirling, whirling as a holy thing.

On the opposite of losing: One spring night in Gainesville, two years ago. In bed, in quiet and prayer. The words surfaced: *Now is the time you begin to get some things back.*

Two days later, a message from Francesca. *I am back.*

Finally, something—someone—had returned. Had become not gone.

When I met up with Francesca soon after this—the first time I had seen her since she sat in our dining room the autumn after we were married and told us she was moving—she handed me a tissue-wrapped package. I opened it. *I felt strongly I was meant to bring you these,* she told me.

Feathers.

Talking with Christianne shortly before leaving for Ireland, a moment when, hearing myself say for the umpteenth time, *If Gary abides,* I stop midstream, say to Christianne, *Maybe I should stop using brackets around that.* What would it be like to unbracket it, to take that phrase out of its parentheses or whatever I've been keeping those words in? How would it be to just take it as a given? *You abide, you abide, you abide.*

—Monday, June 5, 2017—

Oh, my goodness. What a tired and blue day.

I've had trouble getting out of bed the last couple of days, partly because I've stayed up late, but also because I was tired and sad and it just felt too hard to stir myself. And into the tired blueness, or the blue tiredness, I have stirred a strong dose of self-recrimination. Which helps so much.

Now it's nearly one in the afternoon, and I've only just landed in my writing space. Coming here, I walked down the lighted corridor, stopping in front of the bowl-shaped piece of art that hangs on the wall, where I always pause to ask a silent blessing. Tears sprang to my eyes, and I wondered if I would be able to keep it together.

I made my way to my table. Pulled my laptop, glasses, water bottle from my satchel. Sat for a few moments, considering the view, which is nearly entirely green and, today, rain-drenched. The first real day of settling-in, soaking rain we've had since I arrived. I felt the tears coming on again and didn't want them. Then I thought, *Maybe this means I've arrived. I am sad in Ireland.* Not for the first time, just a pronounced sense of it today.

Jim and his family arrived on Saturday morning. He arranged for Geoff, a falconer who lives in Killarney, to come to the hotel for a falconry session with us that afternoon. Geoff, who does lots of work with groups, both at his falconry and on the road, spent an hour and a half with us, and it was a remarkable experience. He brought more birds than I'd imagined—a couple of hawk chicks, two Harris's Hawks, and at least four owls. I called it the clown car of birds of prey; they just kept coming, and they were beautiful.

Geoff flew Arizona, one of the Harris's Hawks, a number of times, enough for us each to have a time or two of her landing on our (thankfully gloved!) hand, which was holding dead chick parts to entice her.

The experience and the timing were especially splendid because just a few days before, I had finished rereading Helen Macdonald's book *H Is for Hawk.* Helen grew up with a fascination with falconry. After her father's sudden death, she acquired a goshawk (named Mabel—great name). Her book is about that experience.

The book fell into my hands on my first trip to Ireland two years ago, in a little bookshop in Kinsale. Though I was (and still am) mostly avoiding "grief lit" books, this one tugged hard at me. I grabbed it as I was packing to come here, thinking it could be an interesting time to reread it.

It was. It is a remarkable book. Hard in places. And strange. And fascinating. And enviable, not only how exquisitely well Helen writes, but also how she finds this practice, and this creature, to focus and absorb and compel her attention in the journey of grief.

Reading it this time around, I had the sense the book was more cohesive than it felt the first time I read it. I'm sure this had everything to do with me and where I was last time and where I am now. I still quite resist the notion that, with respect to grief, the goal is to get *better*. I'm not going to say I'm better. What I do know is I have become more adept at living with the grief. I have become better at figuring out what I need, what's being invited, what helps. Though this started out as one of those days I could scarcely imagine what could help. The sorrow feels so old now. An ancient burden I don't always know how to carry.

This reminds me of something from Jack Gilbert. I came across it again yesterday in revisiting one of his other poems:

Michiko Dead

He manages like somebody carrying a box
that is too heavy, first with his arms
underneath. When their strength gives out,
he moves the hands forward, hooking them
on the corners, pulling the weight against
his chest. He moves his thumbs slightly
when the fingers begin to tire, and it makes
different muscles take over. Afterward,
he carries it on his shoulder, until the blood
drains out of the arm that is stretched up
to steady the box and the arm goes numb. But now
the man can hold underneath again, so that
he can go on without ever putting the box down.

I resist the poem, partly because it is wildly accurate. I know that box—not the same as his, but my own heavy, heavy box of sorrows and grief and rage and weariness. He describes so well the burden of carrying the box. I also resist, even as I understand, how it's not one he anticipates ever putting down. Something judgmental stirs in me, reading this, thinking how unhealthy, how burdensome, and perhaps how futile it is to forever carry that box, that tonnage. And that judgmental part is, I think, stoked by those who come asking questions like, *Are you better now?* Those who, however subtly, convey the expectation, *It's time to move on.*

I don't think I'm stuck. I've written that here before and perhaps simply need to remind myself again. I don't think I'm stuck. Rereading *H Is for Hawk* helped me see that—that it felt like a more cohesive story because I am more cohesive; some things have been piecing themselves together in me. They don't look the same as before, and I don't expect them to. But these shards, these things in me that fell apart with your death, are finding new connections, new ways of holding themselves together in me. Even on a day like this, when they feel so fragile and tenuous and I don't know what to do with them.

Lying in bed this morning, I thought about how there are mornings when I wake and just want to wail. Not even to weep, exactly. But to cry out in pain and rage over having to walk into a new day without you here.

But thinking about that burden Gilbert evokes so clearly and uncomfortably, part of my resistance, too, is that I can't quite imagine ever putting the box down. Don't ever want to put the box down entirely. Don't want to be without the box that is connected with you, even when it is so heavy and tiresome.

I know that the heaviness of grief and the weight of love are not the same thing, though they are deeply intertwined; we grieve because we love. So I don't want to confuse the burden of grief with the graced weight of love, intertwined though they are. Don't want the burden of grief to so occupy my arms, my heart, that I can't keep them open to the love that underpins the grief, that is more solid and enduring than the grief, that is the gold in the ore.

As with so many things in grieving, I have realized it's not a matter of choosing whether or not I will carry the box. I will carry my grief. I don't think it's in me to set it down. But there was an image that came to me during Lent this year, a prayer: that God would open channels into the grief, like a river through stone. I don't pray that the grief be taken away but that God (and you) would work on it, would work through it, would enable it to be something other than a burden that never changes, an impermeable monument to something that has gone.

That image helped; the prayer helped. I was helped also by this: During Lent I came across a piece I had written for All Saints' Day at The Painted Prayerbook several years ago. It closed with the words *May our love be more fierce than our grief.* I began to pray that during Lent. *May my love be more fierce than my grief.* Acknowledging their connection but also trusting that love is more enduring than even the fiercest sorrow.

May my love be more fierce than my grief.

That helped too, along with some other things, like being in Gainesville during the time that spanned my Good Friday birthday and Easter and our anniversary. And making art, especially working with the stitching—the rhythm of that, the ritual of that; letting myself not know quite what I'm doing there but to stitch my way into the unknown, into the mystery. Even in the ongoing weight of the grief, all those things helped open something around my heart. I had a massage session with Francesca during that time. I saw Christianne a few days later. *I felt like I could breathe in a way I hadn't done in a long time*, I told her.

Back to Helen Macdonald. In the spring of this year I did a search to see if she had any new books since *H Is for Hawk*. I came across an interview she did with Tess Taylor of the *Barnes & Noble Review.* Just near the close of the interview, Taylor writes this:

> Macdonald is still bemused by *H Is for Hawk*'s success. "It became a story that was older and bigger than me," she says, "my trip to the underworld and back." She thinks it was good that she was so solitary, both as she grieved and then later as she wrote down that grief. "I think if I'd gone into a version of an American MFA program or something I wouldn't have had the courage to be as weird as I was," she

says. "I mean, there was no one there to tell me that I could not be truly strange.".

I am so glad to have come across this and that she said this—about the courage to be as weird as she was and that there was no one to tell her she could not be truly strange. I shared this with Christianne, and it spurred a great exchange about strangeness—*cultivating a conscious weirdness*, I called it. Part of why I resonated so much with Helen's book is that I resonated with her—her intense focus as a child, which manifested in a fascination with falconry that carried into her adult life. I recognized that intensity, that focus that can sometimes come off as weirdness or can feel strange sometimes even to ourselves, except for when it feels utterly normal, which is most of the time. Birds and then sign language—those were my primary points of utter absorption as a child. And, through it all, and before and beneath it all, the writing—writing about what absorbed and fascinated me. Like for Helen, the intensity present in childhood fascinations carried into my adult life.

In the past year and a half, something of that same fascination and intensity has inhabited my stitching. It's been a place of exploration, something that has deeply engaged my attention and has inspired me to do lots of research and reading and looking at the work of other artists as I find my own language and style with the stitching.

It's taken some curious turns that might seem odd or strange to others. Like a couple months ago, when I started wrapping stones with stitched cloth. I still find myself stitching words and turning them to the inside. Enabling others to read the words is not the point. They are between you and me.

One of the stone wrappings doesn't contain text; it's simply a piece of muslin painted dark with charcoal-colored watercolor, with a seam loosely stitched across its face. Working on it, I thought about when I returned to the studio last year, as I was just beginning to experiment with cloth and stitching and watercolor and paper—the beginnings of the Hidden Book—and found myself thinking about your incision in the hospital, the terrible stitched path that never had time to become a scar, and I began to work on some things that evoked it. But I didn't get very far with that, which was likely just as well. And then, once I started stitching the stones, this one with the incision-like seam came spontaneously, quickly. I'm not sure what to make of it—I'm not sure what to make of any of these stones I've been wrapping (*like a shroud around you*, it occurred to me one day)—but I know it helps.

On an index card in March, I wrote: *Wrapping the stones—this great tenderness toward what has been burdensome.* And this: *Stones—associated with dreaming (Jacob), with resurrection and release.* And this: *Honey from the rock.* ·

Part of what draws me to Ireland—the stones. Ancient and beautiful. How I fell in love with the Burren when I visited two years ago. Longing to return. In that place—how the stone is beautiful in itself, and also how life finds its way amidst the stone. *There are things that grow here that they don't understand how they grow here*, someone told us. *And things that grow here that don't grow anywhere else.*

How the Burren has its own strangeness. Is comfortable in its own landscape. How life knows how to find its way even there. Takes hold there in ways it couldn't do anywhere else.

I seem to be claiming the stone—its ancient capacity for endurance, which I long for in my own life—even as I pray for God to make channels into the stone, into the hard, hard places of my grief.

Which just goes to show that one metaphor is never enough.

Perhaps my pull to the studio is that it helps with both these things. That showing up in the studio—engaging this practice (remember our first phone conversation, when we talked about practicing?), trying to be faithful to showing up even when I don't feel like it—both deepens my endurance and also is a place of opening for me as I let go of deadlines and agendas there.

It is a place where I can cultivate a conscious weirdness. An unconscious weirdness too, I suppose, as I follow threads of thought and curiosity and fascination without trying to impose lots of order—though I still wrestle with that sometimes. Wanting things to look a certain way, to work a certain way, to go more quickly or more smoothly, or not to wrap themselves in so much mystery. That's one of the things I've gotten better at this past year—one of the places where I actually let myself say *better*: giving myself time and space to experiment in the studio, to play, to be there without a big agenda or a deadline or the need to make everything tidy and un-strange. Letting it be that way for as long as necessary. Not imposing a deadline on that, either—on how long I will be in this place of experimenting and exploring and hiddenness. Hoping to always maintain some element of these, though the intensity of them may shift.

I remember—I think it was in the first year after you died—brushing my teeth one day and the words constellating in my head: *Your imagination—this is a place where you can know me.* Later, thinking about that, I thought of the capacity for imagination I've had since childhood, how I've brought that imagination to everything that has absorbed me—the birds, the books, and everything in between. And I decided that if I could bring that same sense of imagination to bear on my life now—this life without you here—that maybe I could live, that drawing on the sense of imagination I've always had would help me make a new life here. I don't know quite how to explain that. It's not about making stuff up, trying to spin into existence what isn't there. But trying to perceive what weaves through this existence, the stuff that is more difficult to see—the things that require art, poetry, dreaming (by both night and day), stories, silence, prayer. And being in the studio, and following the threads of imagination, tugging at them because I know they will lead me to something real.

It occurred to me recently, just within the last month or two, one night when I was in prayer and quiet, that perhaps this experience of creative freedom I'm allowing myself right now is a place of connection with you. Since your death, I have been praying that you are living with utter freedom now, that you are in a place where you can give yourself to writing and performing and creating in all the ways your heart desires. I think of a song from one of the concert recordings for *This Man's Heart*, where you opened by saying this place—this place of writing and performing songs—is where you live and that you're an expatriate in this world.

I pray you are no longer an expatriate, that you are fully at home and fully free where you are.

It came as such a beautiful, powerful thought: that as I move more fully into my own creative freedom, this can be a place of connection with you, who, I pray, are completely free. Moving deeper into this creative freedom not for the sole purpose of connecting with you but knowing that place of connection as part of the gift of this freedom. Wondering if the measure I experience here gives me a small glimpse of the kind of freedom I hope you are living with now.

And why stint with this freedom in this life, even knowing that the freedom will always be only partial? Perhaps seeking it especially because of this fact. Yes to the necessary work that lies outside the studio—there will always be that—but becoming more fierce about seeking this freedom, protecting it, entering into it. Not treating it as a luxury—something I have always been prone to doing, long before you died. In the wake of your death, in the goneness of you from this place, I can afford even less to treat this as a luxury—the artwork, the writing—when it is so clear this is part of how I have survived, and why.

Flow. So much comes down to this: What is the flow that is being invited? How do I release myself into this? All the attendant questions I have been living with: What is the rhythm of life I need? Is this a time to rest or to stretch?

Remembering the words from John O'Donohue about wanting to live like this—fluent, surprised by the river's unfolding.

Fluency. Flow.

Oh, goodness, I haven't told you about Saint Kevin and the

poem. (Sometimes the most pivotal things are the most difficult to capture here.)

A few weeks before I left to come to Ireland the first time, Priscilla handed me a CD. *Solace* by David Whyte. The final poem on the CD is this one:

COLEMAN'S BED

Make a nesting now, a place to which
the birds can come, think of Kevin's
prayerful palm holding the blackbird's egg
and be the one, looking out from this place
who warms interior forms into light.
Feel the way the cliff at your back
gives shelter to your outward view,
then bring from those horizons
all discordant elements that seek a home.

Be taught now, among the trees and rocks,
how the discarded is woven into shelter,
learn the way things hidden and unspoken
slowly proclaim their voice in the world.
Find that far inward symmetry
to all outward appearances, apprentice
yourself to yourself, begin to welcome back
all you sent away, be a new annunciation,
make yourself a door through which
to be hospitable, even to the stranger in you.

See with every turning day,
how each season makes a child
of you again, wants you to become
a seeker after rainfall and birdsong,
watch how it weathers you to a testing
in the tried and true, tells you
with each falling leaf, to leave and slip away,

even from the branch that held you,
to go when you need to, to be courageous,
to be like a last word you'd want to say
before you leave the world.

Above all, be alone with it all,
a hiving off, a corner of silence
amidst the noise, refuse to talk,
even to yourself, and stay in this place
until the current of the story
is strong enough to float you out.

Ghost then, to where others
in this place have come before,
under the hazel, by the ruined chapel,
below the cave where Coleman slept,
become the source that makes
the river flow, and then the sea
beyond. Live in this place
as you were meant to and then,
surprised by your abilities,
become the ancestor of it all,
the quiet, robust and blessed Saint
that your future happiness
will always remember.

I printed the poem and carried it to Ireland in my purse and
for more than a year afterward. It accumulated more text along the
way—notes from conversations I had about the poem with a few
folks and, on the reverse, directions to the pilgrimage site in the
Burren that David Whyte writes about in the poem. The directions are in the hand of Christine Valters Paintner, who wrote them
down as we had lunch in Galway.

(The group tried to go the site. Being good pilgrims, we got
lost along the way, and by the time we made it to the place where
you hike in, it was too late to make a proper visit of it. A regret of

mine from that trip but am trusting it's meant for another time, if it's meant at all, and that, most likely, the poem was the main point, not visiting the place itself.)

So much that struck me about the poem, which crossed my path at such a fortuitous time. It helped provide some language and imagery for the place I sensed myself arriving as I prepared to leave for Ireland. I felt like I had completed some kind of initial arc of grieving, that there was still plenty to do but that I had crossed through a particular stretch of it that culminated on the day we buried your ashes. Leaving for Ireland that first time was the beginning of the next arc. Or turn of the spiral, or whatever shape this path is, if it is any shape at all. If it is even a path.

The saint that really resonates with me in this poem is Saint Kevin. I had heard his story long ago and reacquainted myself with it after receiving this poem. As the story goes, Kevin's oratory was so small that when he stretched out his arms in prayer, he had to reach one hand out the window. One day a bird came to nest in his hand. The saint allowed the bird to stay there and to make a nest. The whole time, Kevin did not move, did not un-house the bird; he continued with his palm outstretched as she built her nest and laid her eggs. Not until the chicks hatched and fledged did he release his hold.

The image lingered with me for months and has not entirely left. Kevin in prayer, reaching out his hands, leaving time and space and room. Letting what comes, come. Making a place for it. I carried that image, prayed with it, hands cupped, wondering what wanted to come and make a nest in me. I would ask you, *Sweetheart, please make a nesting for me, make a nesting in me, make a nesting with me.*

And I found myself in Neidín, this little nest, and found other places and ways of being nested, being homed. They still feel partial in your absence, but somehow you are part of them and perhaps part of their making.

The flow in this poem, so resonant with images of rivers and currents that began to be present after you died. *Stay in this place / until the current of the story / is strong enough to float you out.* These lines, in particular, helped me name the place I was in as I left for Ireland that first time. Leading up to that, I had poured out so much energy doing the online retreats—four of them after you died, which boggles my mind now, but I also see the enormous gift of them, how they provided their own necessary flow, however chaotic, in the first year and a half after you died.

Leaving for Ireland, I had a sense that when I returned, I would need to be home for a while, to stay still. It was not so long after this that I discerned I needed to take a break from doing the online retreats, which came as a surprise but which has been confirmed. Giving me space both to rest in a different way and also to work on new books and be in the studio. I was able to stay in this place and accept that as the invitation for that time. That it wasn't a break from my life or my work but was, in itself, part of the needed flow of the new life that was emerging.

I've had to think about whether I'm still in this place of stillness or if the current of the story actually has begun to float me out. I think it's the latter, though when it began to bear me out, the flow moved me in a different direction than I had anticipated. Early in grief, I had assumed I would, in due time, return to doing public events. Later, when I took time away from doing the online re-treats, I assumed I would be away only perhaps a year, if that.

I don't have those same assumptions anymore. Even as I an-ticipate I'll do online retreats again, will do public events again, I don't know yet when that will be. I've stopped making assumptions about some of the things that were such a part of my life before you died—that they would continue to be part of my life after you died. Given how grief undoes us at a molecular level, it's hard to say what will be preserved from our life before grief entered into it. Though, I should say, I am grateful beyond measure for the strong threads that endure: family and friendships, writing, making art. These particular things that continue—these things I just named—are the things I want my life to be about, and not precisely as before. Though I would so much rather you be here, creating this life anew with me.

I think again of the question you asked, not so long before you died: *Would you be interested in reimagining our life?* I've had this deepening sense, as I have let go of some things this past year and have made substantial decisions about the shape of my life, that your question still holds. That the decisions I'm making now are part of my response to your question—that they are an outflow of the *yes* I gave you at the time, a *yes* whose outcome we could not see. That we are still doing this imagining together.

This too from David Whyte's poem: *Make yourself a door through / to be hospitable, even to the stranger in you.* Last year, I arrived in Ireland feeling like such a stranger in my own life. Could not shake that sensation. When I left, the sensation had loosened a bit, and finally eased. I don't always recognize my life—there are ways it still feels so strange—but I don't feel like a stranger in my life, in my skin, with the sharpness I once did.

—TUESDAY, JUNE 6, 2017—

Sweetheart.

I am having a meltdown and don't know what to do for myself except show up here. I hardly even know what to say. I am feeling sad and inept and lonely and I need to say inept again because I can't even articulate on the page all that is going through my head.

A day of not writing. A day of making bad art. A day of wishing I could go home (or just go on to Sally's, which I'll be doing on the thirteenth, a day and a half after I return home from Ireland), even as part of me doesn't want to leave here. Wondering what I'm doing here and if I've done this trip all wrong.

Last year, coming with expectations about leaving with some finished blessings in hand, then realizing what I needed to do, what the invitation was, was to let it be an archaeology project—to excavate as much as I could and get it down on the page, knowing there would be time to finish and polish the pieces later.

So this time, I set out for Ireland knowing what I wanted to work on—which was mostly this, writing in these pages—but also staying open to whether something else might want to present itself.

Still, I find myself worrying if I'm getting this wrong.

I look at what I've written here and worry if it's enough. And what kind of question is that? What would *enough* look like or feel like?

I'm tired of having breakdowns when I want to be having breakthroughs. I'm aware those often happen together. You were the one who pointed that out to me; that being at my wits' end in the studio, full of despair over what I was working on or what wasn't coming, meant I was on the edge of a breakthrough.

But you're not here to remind me of that. I am so beset by missing you tonight. I am always beset by the missing, but it's reached a point that's wound together with having a hard time knowing what I'm doing here and being so aware that mainly what I'm working on here is a book about you being gone and how I'm trying to survive that.

It is a gorgeous evening here. I am looking out of this window in my room onto this stunning Irish scene. Once again I think how absurd it is to be sad in Ireland. But I am sad because you are not here in this amazing place. And I am in this amazing place because you are not here.

This is one of those times I worry I'm always going to be this sad. One of those times when I don't know what to do with myself.

I think this is just a day where I never really got traction in the way I'd hoped. I had anticipated being up around nine this morning and getting on down to my table and doing some writing and also getting a rough draft of the manuscript printed. I had insomnia and, combined with going into town to run an errand, I didn't arrive till about 1:30 and left shortly after three for a visit with a friend. A productive hour and a half, but that was about it for working on the book today.

I took a stab at working on some stitching this evening. I

brought some supplies—watercolors and linen and things for stitching—and this was the first time I'd pulled them out. I did some watercoloring; wasn't crazy about anything that resulted, but it gave me some things to work with. Started stitching on a piece, and while stitching is generally a helpful thing for my brain and my heart, this piece did not go particularly well. Frustrations with it were part of what sparked the meltdown, which likely was ripe for happening anyway.

I've been watching the moon rise over this landscape of green, green, green—nearly unbroken green except for the bay and the inn beyond. Thinking about what I wrote in *Night Visions* long ago about the moon being whole, even as its light waxes and wanes.

Wanting to believe that still—to believe that about my own life. Knowing there is an underlying wholeness but feeling very tattered. I would also say *scattered* if it weren't such a clanking rhyme with *tattered*. But I do feel scattered and don't know what piece to pick up next. Had hoped the stitching would help—would bring some rhythm and ritual and soothing—and it doesn't feel like it did, except to trigger this meltdown that I hope will ultimately prove helpful but mostly just feels wretched now.

And you? Do you get sad? If you are where I hope you are, I can't really fathom that sorrow is part of your life now (if the Scriptures are to be believed). I worry sometimes that I am disappointing you, that the grief I carry so close to me causes you disappointment or frustration or pain.

And Christianne's question comes to me: *What would his heart be toward you about that?*

I think your heart toward me would not hold disappointment—that there is no room in your heart for that. But you are not here to tell me that.

I'm sure that part of what's stirring in the meltdown and the frustration tonight is the fact of being where I am with *Sparrow*. That it's taking on substance and shape. That while I have quite a way to go with it, I have a much clearer sense of what it's likely to look like and have been working toward that. This is wonderful, and it is also awful. Awful that I have occasion to work on this book. Awful that there will come a time when I will finish it, which I sense will bring another shift between us. I need to be careful of this—the anticipatory grief, which is some of the worst grief there is. The anticipatory grief can be insidious, not least because what shows up at grief's turning points is usually different than what I've anticipated and often holds graces I could not foresee when I was full of dread about something that might not even happen.

Maybe this is a good place to share a poem that came my way sometime in the past couple months. It's by Elizabeth Austen; Peg and Chuck introduced me to her work. She's a former poet laureate of Washington State and has taught at Holden:

WINTER GARDEN

nothing to be done
but wait   that's your whole job
resting and waiting and by god

that's difficult enough   giving up
everything you know
about resilience persistence
winning   listen

when the signal comes
and it always comes
we will all turn over
and begin again   facing the wind
and the place in the clouds
where we last felt sun

I wept when I read the poem. It showed up during a time when I had been struggling once again with whether it was time to rest or to stretch myself in some direction I was resisting. Finally the words materialized in my head one day: *If you can rest, rest.* I wrote the words on an index card. And this, too: *Brooding—cf. Genesis 1.*

The term in Genesis 1:2 often translated as the Spirit *moving* or *hovering* over the waters can also be translated as *brooding*. It occurs to me now that, as Genesis tells it, God doesn't rest until the seventh day of creation, but somehow, in my brain, brooding is connected with resting. That giving myself room to brood, allowing myself time and space to create and breathe and listen and explore and not be hurried about it—that this is a kind of resting, that this is part of what rest means for me right now.

Nothing to be done / but wait, Elizabeth writes; *that's your whole job / resting and waiting and by god / that's difficult enough.*

That sounds like such a luxury, such an extravagance, but what if that's the invitation, the call? What if I can't see what comes next because this is what comes next?

—WEDNESDAY, JUNE 7, 2017—

Last night I dreamed you died. I can remember only fragments, something of a sense that you had died all over again. And for some reason I wasn't there. You said to whoever was with you, *Tell Jan I love her.*

How could I not be there with you?

This dream was not a great outcome of last night's meltdown. Exacerbating the sense of distance. But the *Tell Jan I love her* part— sweetness in that, if dismay and disbelief that I wasn't there to hear it myself.

On another note, this: I saw a sparrow last evening. I was walking back to the hotel from an errand. I started to walk down Main Street—the quickest way—but then turned around, took a left, and headed down Henry Street. A short way down the street, a sparrow flitted in front of me and landed on an awning. I don't think I've seen a sparrow here in Kenmare before. Glad it crossed my path.

Thinking about sparrows. It occurred to me some time ago that for all my childhood fascination with extinct and endangered birds, I have, since your death, been drawn to a bird that is so common. In the States and elsewhere, the sparrow is ubiquitous. It's not even terribly inclined to make its home in lovely spots. I once saw a sparrow making a nest in the first *A* of the sign at Rabba's Fine Foods, down the street from Sally and Craig's, as if it knew an *A* was a good place to begin. An auspicious spot for a home.

There is something comforting in the ubiquity of the sparrow and in its penchant for places that are not always lovely. It is anything but absent. Even as it appears in Psalm 84 as an image of longing, which is a kind of absence (but one that, the psalmist says, leads us home), it turns up again and again in this world, and along my path, as a reminder that solace is not a rarity, is not in danger of disappearing, will not cease to find me even in the unloveliest places in my grief.

Last night, after I finally laid myself down in bed, I found myself thinking I need to begin praying two prayers once again—the ones I wrote about earlier. Asking God to carve channels into my grief. And asking that my love would be more fierce than my grief. Somewhere along the way, probably after Easter, I eased up on those prayers, and did not mean to, and need to return to them. I began last night.

Before that, getting ready for bed and feeling so sore of heart in the wake of the meltdown, I was thinking about *Sparrow* and remembered some words that visited me a while back: *This is not a book. This is a nest.* I needed to be reminded of that last night. That it's not about how much I get written while I'm here (and I already knew that but still got tripped up in it) but about discerning what words need to come and letting them come. I'm not even sure that's quite it, either. What if what needs to come doesn't take the form of words? Or not solely words?

At any rate, it was helpful to remember, *It's not about writing the book. It's about building the nest.*

And what is this nest supposed to look like? Along with the clarity that has come, more questions as well. And, particularly pressing last night, what is the nest supposed to look like *for me*? Because it is, first of all, for me—for you and me—and only after that is it for other people.

The writing has been a shelter—the fact of which is evoked so vividly by being here in Neidín, Little Nest—but also a place of exposure that I have found nearly overwhelming at times. The pain and the beauty of working with the living tissue of our life. Living with the memories and the questions and the stories. Wondering what is yet possible for us and how my life will unfold. What kind of nest I will build or that we will build together.

I was thinking about that this morning. If this book is a nest, and if the process of creating it is a nest as well, then what kind of nest? I've been looking at images of nests the past couple years and have been thinking also of the marvelous program that came on while I was at Mom and Dad's a while back—a *Nature* special about birds and their nests.

There are nests I'm drawn to for their simplicity; I think of a nest I saw, maybe on that special, or in the lovely *Nests* book by Sharon Beals, that was just flat rocks around the eggs. And nests I'm drawn to for how elaborate they are. The bowerbird amazes me still, with what diligence and intricacy it fashions its nest.

Sometime soon after I began writing these pages, I thought of the bowerbird, imagined this writing would be a kind of wooing of you, that I would draw you to me with these words. It occurred to me later that perhaps the opposite was at work as well, that these words draw me to you, keep me connected with you, are part of the nesting and home we can still make together, even as we seek to be present to the place where we each are, wherever that is. Days I can scarcely recognize or describe the place where I am now, let alone imagine where you are.

I wonder: Was it immediately recognizable to you, the place where you are now? Did you know yourself immediately at home, the sparrow arrived? Or has this home, taking you in so unexpectedly soon, taken getting used to? Whatever the answer, what has helped you in the place where you are now? I don't think that question has ever occurred to me till now. Was help even at issue? Do you move with such freedom now that *help* isn't even a category that registers for you—something you are beyond needing?

In any case, if help was something you needed, I am curious about what helped and whether it's something available to me here, in such sore need of help as I am.

—Thursday, June 8, 2017—

I dreamed of you again last night. Less fraught than the night before, when I dreamed you had died and I wasn't there. Two pieces I remember, maybe from different dreams. One, just a small fragment: waltzing with you to "The Blue Danube." Waltzing fairly dramatically; we were having much fun with it.

In the second dream, I was at a festival or some such thing. I was wandering around the festival; it was partly on the water, and there were lots of docks where people were hanging out. I finally ran into you. You were costumed for a show you were performing in. We went on from there together.

Well, if they weren't fraught-with-meaning dreams, at least it was wonderful to see you last night. And that, in those dreams, you weren't dying. It was fun, in the first dream, being silly with you. And in the second dream to know that you were performing, that you were involved in a production.

In recent months I have found myself thinking about you and theater, how important Tropical Theatre and Theatre Downtown were to you, what presence you had on the stage, how leading up to your death you had been working on a story that was providing background material for a show you wanted to create for you and Emile to do at the Fringe Festival one day.

I remember how you talked about the worlds it was possible to create in the theater. I remember what your voice sounded like when you talked about that. And I wonder if you're doing theater now, if that's something you feel drawn to do, and if, in that place, you are creating worlds even beyond what you had dreamed of here. What stories might you be telling and enacting and dreaming there?

The dreams last night helped also because even as I've been writing in these pages while I've been in Ireland, I have been feeling the weight, the expanse, of the distance between us. Having a hard time sometimes sensing you near and sometimes wondering if I'm merely talking to myself in these pages. I think of a conversation I had with Christianne a good while ago, when I was feeling that distance on another occasion. I told her I hoped the sensation was because there's nothing between you and me that happens at the surface anymore. Not that anything ever happened at a surface level between us; that was true right from the start. You have gone deeper and deeper into my bones, and that's where the conversation happens between us, at those levels that are deep and where movement can seem so subtle.

So on the heels of dreaming you had died, it came as a gift to glimpse you in the dreaming last night, to waltz with you and to be somewhere you were performing. Just to see your face and feel some normalcy between us, when nothing is normal.

I pray I'm not dreaming this up, that the reason—or one of the reasons—you sometimes feel so distant is because the conversation, that mysterious exchange between us that the word *conversation* doesn't begin to capture because it's only partly about words, happens so far beneath the surface.

That was part of my anguish a couple nights ago. Having such a hard time hearing. Not knowing how I should be listening. Remembering how I sensed you, early on, wanting me to know, *You don't have to work at it—to hear me.* Not always knowing how to relax into that conversation. And not always knowing how to have the conversation while also listening for my life, how it wants to unfold here, in this place where you are not, where you are no longer in the flesh. But sensing also that listening for my life and listening for you are not two different things, as I sometimes feared early on. They are part of the same movement. One that requires a sort of yoga that is difficult and beautiful.

Writing this, I remember the yoga classes I took, how the instructor told us to pay attention to our breathing, to breathe deeply, to not stop breathing. I sometimes forget that now—in the listening, in the discerning, in the working, in all that's involved in creating a new life that still somehow involves you—to keep breathing. To breathe deeply. To not stop breathing.

What would it mean to relax into this conversation now? Here, in this beautiful place I have been given and in the places that will come along on this strange path, what would it mean to take your words—that I don't have to work at it—to heart all over again? That you are there. That the conversation is there. That we have learned a lot of the language already, and that while there's tons still to learn, we have made a beginning.

Which reminds me—the sense that visited me one day, maybe in the second year after you died, after a string of synchronicities and some curious things that were stirring, you wanting me to know, *This is all prelude.* That there were wonders to come, of which these synchronicities and curiosities were only a foretaste. It made me smile at the time. *This is all prelude.* The kind of thing you would want me to know.

Circling back to my prayer that my love would be more fierce than my grief. *That deeper current,* I wrote on an index card last spring, during Lent, after I began to pray for this. Knowing that the love and the grief couldn't be entirely separated but having a sense, a knowing, that the love lives deeper than the grief. Wanting to connect with that current, the flow of the love that is stronger and more enduring than the grief. On that card I also wrote: *Becoming still enough to sense it. Or being willing to dive that deep. Is it stillness or movement that's required?*

I wrote this too: *Learning to breathe the water. Seeing the creatures that live only at that depth, in their wonder and strangeness.* Taken by that image. That perhaps the flow that's being invited for me is not only about finding the current that will bear me along, though that's crucial (I think of the David Whyte poem and also of the wondrous dream in which you were bearing me along on a river), but also being willing to dive, to find what's beneath the surface and to connect with those currents. Imagining the worlds there that contain both wonders and strangeness. Not assuming I know or will recognize everything that inhabits it, and taking that as gift—even as I recall the words you would always tell me when I set out on a plane trip without you (which became increasingly rare in later years, flying without you): *Keep your wits about you*. There are dangers in the deep, along with the wonders.

It rained earlier today, then turned into a gorgeous evening. I took a walk—a beautiful time of day for it. Walked through part of Reenagross Park, behind the hotel, and took the path to where it comes out on Shelbourne Street. Hung a left and walked down to the small park on Kenmare Bay. Sat there for a while, watching the light on the water and a quartet of dogs having a blast down the way, chasing sticks their people threw into the water.

The gills of grief. Thinking just now about breathing the water, about diving and learning how to breathe underwater—how do we learn to do this when we are drowning in sorrow? Perhaps it takes that relaxing, letting ourselves learn how not to struggle, so that those gills appear on their own—that mechanism, that capacity that enables us to move through the worlds for which we were not very well designed.

It occurs to me that it takes a certain unburdening of ourselves in order to do this, a streamlining, letting go of what keeps us from moving through the waters.

Maybe this is just a different way of talking about the underworld—the strange journey into other realms that grief propels us toward. We have to learn what it takes to pass through those realms—to identify and complete the tasks, discern what offering is required, or figure out the riddle. Sometimes it's not about coming up with the right answer but with the right question. I think of Perceval in the Grail legends and the suffering he goes through because, at a crucial point, he fails to ask the right question.

In the legends, one version of the Grail question is *What ails thee?* It strikes me as an apt question for my life right now. What ails me? Not quite in the sense of *What is wrong with you?* Though there are days the question does feel like that. What is wrong with me? Why can't I get it together? Will I always feel this way? Despite those days, the question seems more like *What's the wound, and what medicine does it need?*

I am keen not to see grief as pathological, as it's sometimes considered, like it's a problem that needs to be fixed. But I remember a time after your death—maybe toward the end of the first year or the beginning of the second—when I said to Maru, *I feel like I have a wasting disease.* That was the best way I could describe it. The grief was so grinding, and I felt so unlike the person I had been before your death.

This makes me think of—and pull out of my satchel—one of the pieces of paper I brought with me on this trip. It's a reservation confirmation for the clinic I went to after I broke my foot, with notes I scribbled onto it one night during dinner at No. 35 last year. Among those notes, this: *How I could feel myself becoming another person, and hating that.* I remember the sorrow and dismay of writing that. How keenly I could feel myself becoming someone other than who I was before you died. Could feel myself becoming Jan After Gary's Death, Jan Having to Make a New Life, Jan Learning How to Be in This World Without You. Even as I recognized the graces and could take some measure of solace in making decisions that helped me move into this life, I hated the fact of it, hated having to become someone other than who I had been.

I wrote this, too, on that piece of paper: *Now—making some peace with the person I am becoming—but still feeling like such a stranger in my own life. How do I find something familiar—territory that is more familiar to me? Not familiar, exactly—but where I don't feel like so much of a stranger in my own skin, my own being. How do I settle into this new skin? How do I fit my frame around these bones that are—literally—shifting?*

June 10, I noted on the paper. Almost exactly a year ago. Grateful, now, to be feeling like less of a stranger in my life. But never without the missing, never without the ache. That's a huge part of the answer to the question of what ails me. I ache.

I think of what I wrote in *The Cure for Sorrow*—that, ultimately, love is the remedy for grief. And there I am, spiraled back around to my own medicine.

—FRIDAY, JUNE 9, 2017—

Another day of having a hard time getting out of bed and having to congratulate myself at each step along the way. *I'm out of bed. In the shower. Drying my hair. Dressed.*

And in the midst of breakfast, looking out on the beautiful landscape that today is gray and misty, thinking about how sad I am and feeling bad about how sad I am, this thought: *If I could just figure out what to do.* Bursting into tears over my peanut butter sandwich because I feel so keenly that desire to *do,* to figure out some way to be in a different place than I am now, and also feeling the weight, the burden and futility, of that thought. Aware that the invitation right now seems not to be about doing. Thinking again about Elizabeth Austen's poem: *That's your whole job / resting and waiting and by god / that's difficult enough.*

But still I feel the need to do something. Not sure I am built for simply sitting around.

What does this waiting look like? And what am I waiting *for*?

Thinking again of yoga. How it asks us to stretch without straining. To keep breathing. To learn how to hold the pose without hurting ourselves.

Thinking also of the question that surfaced last night—the Grail question *What ails thee?* Carrying that question still. I am aware of how self-absorbing grief can be, how, on top of my natural introversion, the grief often requires extra measures of effort to see beyond myself and connect with others. Having to navigate that ongoing discernment about how I connect while also having the space I need. Without becoming utterly absorbed in my own self, in my own grief and sorrow. Wanting to attend to the grief without letting it consume me.

I have felt such a sense of futility at points this week. Self-recrimination for how hard it's been to get out of bed some mornings (self-recrimination being such a great way to begin the day). Disappointment and frustration over some of the challenges with the rhythm of writing. Stress as I think about some things I need to take care of before I leave this Sunday. Nothing big in itself. But so often it's the little things that daunt me—the accumulation of them, particularly when there's a deadline at the other end.

This morning, as I was trying to scale back my sense of guilt at feeling sad in Ireland, I found myself thinking, *I'm not even good at being sad in Ireland.* Feeling again that I was doing even the sadness wrong. But then it occurred to me, *Ireland! What a fantastic place to be sad!* I've commented before on my sense that Ireland is good at absorbing sorrow, and I have experienced it as a place of solace for myself, but when I fall into these especially sad places, as I have this week, I don't always stop to think about what I might turn to in this landscape, in this place. Particularly on a gray day such as this, it seems a good question.

Another question comes back to me, one of the questions that surfaced as I was preparing to talk with Christianne about *Sparrow* shortly before I left: *What graces do I need to ask for as I work on this book? What sustenance do I need?* This feels connected to some of what surfaced for me last night with the *What ails thee?* question: *What medicine does my grief need right now?*

I've been thinking again about the conscious weirdness I wrote about in connection with Helen Macdonald's book. Maybe this too is part of the grief medicine I am needing.

There is an inherent weirdness to grief. It is such a strange ride, turning us inside out, making us feel like a stranger in our life. Nothing is normal. Part of the appeal of finding something a little odd or offbeat—falconry, say, or threads I've been following in the studio—is that it meets the inherent strangeness of grief with its own weirdness. Like a homeopathic remedy, taking a dose of something that would be damaging in larger doses and using that as part of the cure. *Like cures like*, I read when I looked up a definition for *homeopathy* just now. *Similia similibus curentur.*

It can be so easy to get caught up in what grief *should* look like that it can be difficult to let ourselves take this different approach, to engage it with all the imagination and resources we have at hand, including things that might seem weird or strange to those who aren't actually living inside our grief.

Within reason, of course. I know the strangeness of grief can take disturbing twists and turns, can lure us into reaching for things to dose it with (often literally; it's no surprise people in grief are susceptible to substance abuse) to tamp down the weirdness and pain of it.

And that stirs something for me—thinking about the temptation to find shortcuts that will dial back the weirdness and pain of grief. I am remembering when I was working with the story of Eve for *In the Sanctuary of Women.* Writing about that moment when, having taken the fruit, having eaten it, Eve and Adam find their eyes opened, and they see and know as they have not done before. They turn away from God and, somehow, from themselves. Across the centuries, we have thought this was because their seeing caused them shame. But I began to wonder, working with that story, if they turned away not for shame but because what they saw was so stunning. That Eden was overwhelming. That opening their eyes to the beauty of that earth and of their own selves was unbearable.

That's part of what grief does, in an intensely painful, perverse kind of way: it reveals to us the wonder of what we have known, the beauty of the world and of the love we have lived with. And the pain comes not only because the person who stirred that love (*you, you, you*) has died but because the absence of that person has a way of revealing the intensity and wonder of the love that was present and has not entirely left.

This deepening sense, since your death: How beautiful you

were. How beautiful you are. Without glossing over, varnishing, overlooking anything. Simply the beauty of you and of your love. Seeing this more and more clearly. The pain of this; the wonder of this.

Praying to keep my eyes open, even to the aching beauty. Perhaps this is part of the grief medicine: letting myself know that beauty and that love, not only as things of the past, as the stuff of memories, but woven deeply—how deeply—into the present. Here and now.

—SUNDAY, JUNE 11, 2017—
En route

I have left Ireland and am bound for home.

At dinner last night, a friend asked something about how my time in Kenmare had been. *Textured* was one of the words I used. I have been dismayed by the sadness that visited me but so grateful for the sweetness and the graces that wove through the time and met the sadness with some solace.

I've been watching the landscape much of the time that I've been in the air today—when I can see the landscape—and sometimes watching the clouds and the water as well, noticing their landscape too. Struck by the presence of the patterns that appear in the crossing of the landscape. The rivers a particular point of fascination, the artful twisting of them. Knowing that the twisting and turning is how the river finds its flow—that it does not force its path and that straight is hardly ever the way things run.

For all the beauty of the land and the water and the intertwining of the two, one of the most compelling landscapes of the day was the runway at Logan Airport in Boston. As we were preparing to take off, I noticed the pavement and the many places it had been repaired. The repairs, the black of the asphalt against the gray pavement, made fantastic lines. *The calligraphy of repair*, I thought to myself as we taxied, the lines picking up speed. I wanted to get into the studio immediately, to get my hands on paper and black ink or paint, and to travel those lines, to trace that calligraphy.

As I've been stitching over this past more-than-a-year and looking at the work of textile artists, I've been fascinated by what's sometimes called *visible mending*—repairs that are made without trying to hide the fact of the damage, not trying to erase what has been torn by misadventure or worn by time and use. Kintsugi is an example of visible mending that folks often lift up as an example of how beauty can come from brokenness, and that's a striking example, but some of my favorite images of visible mending are ones where the materials of repair are as humble as what they are repairing. I'm thinking especially of methods such as darning and how artful that can be. I have also been gathering images of other kinds of repairs. Cracked Victorian plates held together by staples. Wooden utensils mended with tin. Things that seem all the more beautiful by the care someone has given to salvaging what might otherwise have been thrown away.

I don't want to be romantic about it, or trite. Damage is damage. It is painful, it can take horrid forms, and the fact that sometimes we are able to bring beauty out of it doesn't excuse the damage or make it acceptable or worth the pain. When some kind of repair can take place—which doesn't mean making it look like it used to—that is a wonder. And if beauty becomes manifest in the repair—that is a wonder too, though not the main goal.

I remember when, sometime after your death, I found myself thinking, *I can't change the fact of my grief, but I can make it beautiful.* Saying that to Maru one night, and hearing her say back, *You don't have to make it beautiful. Just let it be.* And while I think I wasn't wrong to want to bring some beauty to the grief, I think she's right that it's not the main goal and that any beauty that emerges in my grief isn't all dependent on me, on my efforts to wrest some loveliness from the awfulness of your absence.

The fact of not trying to make something look like it used to—that's so much of what draws me to visible mending. Acknowledging that repair isn't about hiding what is broken, damaged, cracked, frayed, torn. It's about working with it. Bringing attention and care. Allowing ourselves to be present to the damage and to ask for the graces we need to be part of how its repair takes place. Not turning away from the brokenness; keeping our eyes open to it and also to the beauty and wholeness that love to slip in and take us by surprise.

This reminds me of a day when the words surfaced: *Solace is your job now.* How it felt like something you might want me to know. And that it meant—means—both finding solace for myself—what that looks like, how to ask for it, how to allow it to come—and also offering solace to others. That the invitation—the call, the vocation—includes both of these movements: letting myself look for and receive solace, and passing along the gift of it to others.

How this is the job now: asking for solace, finding the tools and mediums and practices by which it comes. Not by dint of effort but by opening myself to it. Placing myself in its path. Following its flow. Becoming part of that current.

Those lines at Logan. How they looked like an ancient language and also like a map. How they had their own kind of flow. I want to learn that lettering, that cartography. I want to write that calligraphy of repair, to follow the lines by which a new world is found.

—Monday, June 26, 2017—
Toronto

Then there was this on the way home from Logan Airport.

You know how much I am not someone who enjoys long chats with strangers on airplanes. How I put up my invisible force field in hopes that, beyond being cordial, I will not become ensnared in a conversation, particularly since being on an airplane usually means I'm tired and just want to savor not having to do anything for the length of a flight—that I am unreachable and don't need to respond to anyone or accomplish anything for that period of time except to let myself be moved from one place to another.

I was by the window during this flight home, able once again to watch the landscape sometimes and glad to be left to my coming-home-from-Ireland thoughts. I had noticed the woman next to me was reading a popular Bible commentary, but we hadn't exchanged any conversation.

Toward the end of the flight, she leaned over and asked, *Are you American?* When I told her yes, she pointed to a place on the page she had been reading and asked, *Can you tell me what this means? 'Nagging wife'?* She was in the book of Proverbs, evidently. I said something about scolding and shook my finger.

I learned she was from Brazil. She told me her name.

Racia? I asked. We were sitting near the engines, and between their loud noise and her gentle voice, I was not sure I had understood.

Gracia, she said. *Grace.*

She told me she was a neurosurgeon.

I was sitting next to a neurosurgeon named Grace. When I realized this, I could not help but return to the hospital waiting room, at the moment your neurosurgeon entered and told us the terrible news that felt anything but graced. And now, returning from Ireland, I was in the company of a neurosurgeon named Grace. It felt important, that I needed to pay attention to this.

We had a remarkable conversation, of which, in typical fashion, I remember only pieces. She said she became a neurosurgeon because of her mother, who was terribly ill when Gracia was growing up, and died. I told her a little about you and about your surgery. She commented on what we have done, what we have become— she because of her mother, me because of you. How we have both worked in healing vocations because of the brokenness we have experienced.

We were chosen for this, she said to me.

I don't know if that's true. I don't particularly want to believe this is true, that God would choose people in such a cruel fashion. Again my disdain for the notion that there is a larger picture at work that justifies the suffering we see and experience in our corner of the canvas. I can only say here that, in that moment, amid my resistance, her words rang in me. They did not ring true or false; they simply rang, inviting me to notice. As with so much in the wake of your dying, I neither believe nor disbelieve this idea, that we could be so chosen.

Gracia asked what book I was working on now. I told her a little about *Sparrow*. She began to sing to me: *I'd rather be a sparrow than a snail...*

"El Condor Pasa." The song that Simon and Garfunkel sang approximately a zillion years ago, based on a song that originated on Gracia's continent.

I wish I could remember more of our conversation. Those gaps, again, that are so present in my grieving. But I remember how it felt, the wonder of it, as if Ireland were getting in one more moment of synchronicity. I don't think remembering the particulars was the point of that encounter, anyway, so much as the sheer fact that on my journey home from Ireland, I encountered a neurosurgeon named Gracia. Grace. A woman who knows how fragile we are, how easily we are broken; one who also knows what can come through the breaking—the grace and new life that pass through the rupture—if we learn to open ourselves to it.

Gracia and I touched down in Orlando. She would have a long wait for her late-night flight home to Brazil. As we parted, she sang to me again: *I'd rather be a sparrow than a snail...*

She blew me a kiss and disappeared into the crowd.

Two days after my conversation with Gracia, I was in another country once again, this time in Canada for a visit with Sally and her family.

One day, on a walk in their neighborhood early in my stay, I noticed the street had repairs like the ones I saw on the runway in Boston. I began taking pictures, thinking to follow these lines for inspiration when I returned home to my studio. I crossed the street to shoot the lines from a different angle, and that's when I heard them. Coming from the direction of a paved path alongside a creek, the chorus was one I recognized.

Sparrows.

I walked down the path toward the sound. There were more sparrows than I had ever seen together. Many of them were clustered along a chain-link fence and the trees nearby. Some of the sparrows squeezed through the gaps in the fence—they could easily have flitted over it—and I found it difficult to shake the sense they were playing.

The next day, I set out for a walk, thinking to look for the sparrows. I was nearly back to the house before I realized I must have missed the path by the creek. I retraced my steps and finally saw it: I had found the path the first time only when I crossed the street to look at the repairs from a different direction.

I did not find the flock that day, nor in the days that followed. I returned to the creek many times. Though I could hear sparrows around me and would see them in ones or twos nearly every time I stepped outside, I never saw the flock again.

Postscript

I am cautious about drawing conclusions or imposing closure on something that will never be entirely finished.

There is no escaping the awful fact of it: the sparrow fell. I know of no explanation, no justification, no meaning or larger picture that will make sense of it. I will forever be gazing into that gap, that absence, tracing the shimmering outline of the broken sparrow, the brilliance that passed into this world and out of it bearing my husband's name.

What I know is that sometimes, something slips through the gap. The absence sings, coaxing us to trust there is more than emptiness, more than an eternal void that opens where a life has been.

We are attended. We are accompanied. We are asked to open our eyes, our hearts, to the grace of it, that we might bear witness not only to the fall of the sparrow but also to what follows it: the aching mystery that comes to sing in our bones, the presence that releases us into this living and into this world but also, with wondrous strangeness, goes with us still, making a nest in us and helping us find our way home.

Acknowledgments

In the un-homing that came with Gary's death, I have found powerful solace in the sheltering of family, friends, and colleagues who have helped make this book and my life possible. For their part in this sheltering, I am grateful to Peg Carlson-Hoffman, Chuck Hoffman, Jim Knipper, Maru Ladròn de Guevara, Martha Plank, Barbie Boyd, Karen Weatherford, Kathy Craven, Emily Wray, Cindy Van Lunen, Brenda Lewis, Priscilla Santiago, Janice Elsheimer, Dorri Sherrill, Carolyn Mathis, Lesley Brogan, Carol Wilson, Leslee Lyndon Wray, Linda Ellis, Ronda Banner, and Sarah Wolking. Many of them read the manuscript in progress.

Particular thanks go to our remarkable family: my parents, Judy and Joe; my sister and brother-in-law, Sally and Craig; my brother and sister-in-law, Scott and Lacinda; Gary's son, Emile; his father and stepmom, Harold and Dee; and his brothers and sisters-in-law, Greg and Doreen, Jeff and Suzanne, and Jon and Heather.

It is a joy to include poetry and other pieces that found their way to me with mysterious timing after Gary's death. I am grateful to those who have allowed their work to appear here, oftentimes with a kindness and generosity that came as a grace. I am especially thankful for Sally Smith, who coordinated the permissions process. I am grateful also to Amanda Quain, who was a marvelous proof-reader.

My extraordinary editor and friend, Christianne Squires, knew the heart of *Sparrow* from the beginning and was instrumental in helping shape the nest this book has become.

I could not have anticipated the strange and wondrous occasions of synchronicity that would keep returning me to the town of Kenmare, Ireland, where parts of *Sparrow* were written. The hospitality and good cheer of its kind folks are enduring blessings.

And I am forever grateful for Gary, whose sheltering spirit endures.

Permissions

Page 78: O Antiphon from *Meditations on the O Antiphons*. Copyright © 1962 by The Sisters of St. Benedict; The Liturgical Press; Collegeville, MN 56301.

Page 90: "Grief," and "Grief" from BOOK OF HOURS: POEMS by Kevin Young, copyright © 2014 by Kevin Young. Used by permission of Alfred A. Knopf, an imprint of the Knopf Doubleday Publishing Group, a division of Penguin Random House LLC. All rights reserved.

Page 91: Excerpt from the musical *Big Fish*. Book by John August, based on the novel by Daniel Wallace and the Columbia Motion Picture. Used by permission of John August.

Pages 92–93: Quote from p. 106 from BREAD FOR THE JOURNEY: A DAYBOOK OF WISDOM AND FAITH by HENRI J.M. NOUWEN. Copyright © 1997 by Henri J.M. Nouwen. Reprinted by permission of HarperCollins Publishers.

Page 101: Matthew Zapruder, excerpt from "Aglow" from *Come on All You Ghosts*. Copyright © 2010 by Matthew Zapruder. Reprinted with the permission of The Permissions Company, LLC on behalf of Copper Canyon Press, www.coppercanyonpress.org.

Page 104: Excerpt from pp. 211–12 from BEAUTY: THE INVISIBLE EMBRACE by JOHN O'DONOHUE. Copyright © 2004 John O'Donohue. Reprinted by permission of HarperCollins Publishers.

From *Divine Beauty* by *John O'Donohue*
Published by *Bantam Press*
Reprinted by permission of The Random House Group Limited.
© 2003

Page 109: "Fluent" from CONAMARA BLUES: POEMS by

First published 2015 by
Veritas Publications

7-8 Lower Abbey Street
Dublin 1, Ireland
publications@veritas.ie
www.veritas.ie

Page 170: "I Hear Nothing in My Ear" from *The Soul of Rumi: A New Collection of Ecstatic Poems*, translated by Coleman Barks. Copyright © 2001 by Coleman Barks. Used by permission of the author.

Page 177: "Even" from THE BIRD CATCHER by Marie Ponsot, copyright © 1998 by Marie Ponsot. Used by permission of Alfred A. Knopf, an imprint of the Knopf Doubleday Publishing Group, a division of Penguin Random House LLC. All rights reserved.

Pages 189–190: "Hiding" excerpts from *Consolations: The Solace, Nourishment, and Underlying Meaning of Everyday Words* by David Whyte, © Many Rivers Press, Langley, WA USA. Printed with permission from Many Rivers Press, www.davidwhyte.com.

Pages 215–216: Excerpt from TO BLESS THE SPACE BETWEEN US: A BOOK OF BLESSINGS by John O'Donohue, copyright © 2008 by John O'Donohue. Used by permission of Doubleday, an imprint of the Knopf Doubleday Publishing Group, a division of Penguin Random House LLC. All rights reserved.

From ***BENEDICTUS*** by ***JOHN O'DONOHUE***
Published by ***Bantam***
Reprinted by permission of The Random House Group Limited.
© 2007

Pages 222–223: "In the Museum of Lost Objects" from *Love, An Index* by Rebecca Lindenberg, copyright © 2012 by Rebecca Lindenberg. Used by permission of the author.

Page 227: "Michiko Dead" from THE GREAT FIRES: POEMS,

Songs

Some of the lyrics that appear in Sparrow *were released on albums by Garrison Doles. They are as follows:*

Page xv: "I Will Be a Sparrow" from *Draw Us Closer*

Page 27: "The Unused Portion" and "Are We Abandoned" from *One Man*

Page 29: "This Man's Heart" from *This Man's Heart*

Page 33: "The Osprey Circles" from *Whenever I'm With You*

Pages 55–56: "Raise This Hour" from *Draw Us Closer*

Page 113: "All I Want Is You" from *Whenever I'm With You*

Page 162: "Hymn of the Stone" from *One Man*

Pages 219–220: "O There Is a Shelter" from *House of Prayer*